AF482375

This important book, now emended and further enriched, is a key – or to use a current parlance, an avatar, for the Kapampangan entity in search of its genuine past and is an inspiration for other entities in similar struggle. Craftily interspersed in the pages are in-depth historical backgrounds about this ancient script already lost due to centuries of suppression and inutility – and technical yet friendly guides on how it can be learned again by any Kapampangan (or anybody, actually) interested in the cause of an authentic cultural renaissance after centuries of colonial domination. Luid ing Kapampangan!

Lino L. Dizon
Commissioner, National Historical Commission of the Philippines

Kulitan is a book of love, for language, history, culture, traditional and modern interpretations of the script, and, most importantly, for the Kapampangan people. May it inspire present and future generations.

Tom Hoogervorst
Royal Netherlands Institute of Southeast Asian and Caribbean Studies

Every minority culture with its own writing system needs a Mike Pangilinan—someone knowledgeable, passionate, and committed, who knows that to understand and promote a traditional language—whether spoken, written or both—is to understand and promote an entire people.

Tim Brookes
Book Author, Sculptor and An Advocate for Endangered Scripts

In our quest for a national identity, we often forget that cultural diversity adds much more beauty, color, flavor and spice to our lives. The efforts of Siuálâ ding Meángûbie to save the Kapampangan language helps keep us all from getting lost in that ugly gray bland shadow of homogeneity.

Nordenx (Norman de los Santos)
Founder, Anak Bathala Project Creative Director
BHM Games Studio, Corp

This book is unquestionably a remarkable achievement in research on KULITAN, the indigenous Kapampangan script. It is a valuable reference not only for Kapampangans and scholars and students of Kapampangan but also for anyone interested in Asian writing systems.

Dr. Naonori Nagaya
National Institute for Japanese Language and Linguistics

Siuálâ ding Meángûbie has written a prodigious book which I believe is a classic in linguistics, anthropology, history, etc. The product of a brilliant mind, his achievement in writing his first book is akin to Padre Anselmo J. Fajardo's revitalization of the Kapampangan language and literature through his play Don Gonzalo de Cordova in 1831. Siuálâ ding Meángûbie is not only the 'Father of Filipino Calligraphy' but is now, as he has been – but hitherto unregarded, the foremost authority on Kapampangan language and culture. A hidden national treasure: "Nobody is a prophet in his own land.

Dr. Luciano P.R. Santiago
Genealogist, Historian, Researcher, Writer

KULITAN

National Library of the Philippines CIP Data

Pangilinan, Michael Raymon M.
An Introduction to Kulitan : The Indigenous Kapampangan Script / Michael Raymon M. Pangilinan. — Angeles City, Pampanga Sínúpan Singsing Book Publishing, [2023], c2023.
pages ; cm

1. Kapampangan language — Writing. 2. Kapampangan language — Etymology. 3. Kapampangan language — Phonology. I. Title.

499.21717 PL5994.P36 2023 P320230177

ISBN: 978-621-96825-0-3 (Softbound/Paperback)

Printed in the Philippines.

Proof reading by Robert LaRue

Book design by Soleil Ilyanna L. Cruz

Kulitan graphics by Albert Jonah M. Medina

Cover design by Justin C. Lacson

First Edition, 2012
Second Edition, 2023

Published by Sínúpan Singsing Book Publishing
Angeles City, Pampanga, Philippines 2009

An Introduction to

KULITAN

The Indigenous Kapampangan Script

2nd edition

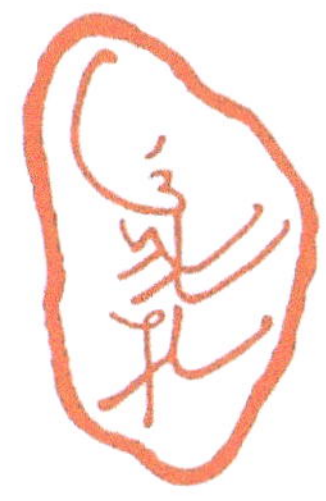

Siuálâ ding Meángûbié
Michael Raymon M. Pangilinan

Sínúpan Singsing Book Publishing
Angeles City, Pampanga, Philippines

BÍLUNGAN
Table of Contents

PÁMAGLÁBUNG

SÚSUG

ING LÚPA NING AKLAT
About the Cover

Ing Kabiasnang Kapampángan

É mé pánintunan ing Kabiasnang Kapampángan karéng libru ampó pang méstra. É mé ákit iti karing ápat nang súluk ning iskuéla. Aláyu iti karing táwung tituládu, ó karétang mésábi móng pantas.

Ing Kabiasnang Kapampángan, atí yu king Aldó ampóng Búlan, king Uran ampóng Amian, atí king Súnis da ring Áyup, king Lawiswis da ring Kuáyan, king mámalimpúyut a Alaúlî, king Gabun a mámié Kálam.

Iniá pantunan mé iti karing Mámálut at Mánasan, karing Pandé at Anluágî, karing Mánalaksan ampóng Mangkukúran, karing Mánayî at Magkakari.

Damdaman mé iti karing Sagakgak da ring Ának ampó king pasiuk na ning mágpastul damúlag, at king pasaldak nang pangisnáwa ning sísintang dalága.

É mé iti babásan, nung é dápat mé iting damdaman, takman at biáyan.

The short Kapampángan essay above speaks about the true nature of indigenous Kapampángan knowledge, that it cannot be found in books or institutions, but in the life of the people themselves and their relationship with their homeland.

On the background is a picture of the idyllic Kapampángan rural life ~ a farmer riding leisurely on the back of a water buffalo amidst a vast rice field. Towering above them is the imposing figure of the sacred mountain of Aláya.

Superimposed upon this idyllic picture is the lyrics of the first stanza of the iconic Kapampángan song, *Atin ku pung Singsing*, written in Kulitan by the author himself. In Kapampángan philosophy, SINGSING 'the ring' is the symbol of ALÁYA 'the Kapampángan Spirit,' from which this indigenous knowledge radiates from.

Justin Calmâ Lacson, carefully weaves all these elements and blends them with the three colors sacred to the Kapampángan people. These colors represents the god of the sacred mountain of Aláya, Ápung Sínukuan ~ KUNDÍMAN 'crimson' is the color of fire and the color of blood, representing both the destructive and creative power of the sun, Ápung Sínukuan; GINTÛ 'gold' is the color of nobility and perfection. ALUNTIANG 'green' is the color of rebirth and regeneration, that comes in the form of the healing rain after the destructive fire and lightning of the sun, Ápung Sínukuan.

Note: The word "Kulitan" written in Kulitan was originally brushed by Kulitan writer Albert Jonah Pángilínan-Mallari Medina, while the lyrics of the iconic song "Atin ku pung Singsing" in Kulitan were originally written by the author Michael Raymon Táyag-Manalóto Pángilinan.

TAGULÁLING
Dedication

Laús lúb ku yang tataguláling iting katipúnan ding kanákung pámanialiksik king kékatámung Amánang Súlat karing kanákung súgîng pípunpúnan ~ Pángilinan, Mánalóto, Língat, Táyag, Púnû, Limcolioc (林高柳*), Disón (*李孫*), Toledáno, Imibe (*齋部*) ~ a king úlî ra ámána ku iting sablâng kabiasnan* [I wholeheartedly dedicate this compilation of my research on our *Amánang Súlat* (inherited script) to the spirit of my ancestors ~ Pángilinan, Mánalóto, Língat, Táyag, Púnû, Limcolioc (林高柳), Disón (李孫), Toledáno, Imibe (齋部) ~ from whom I have inherited all this learning.]

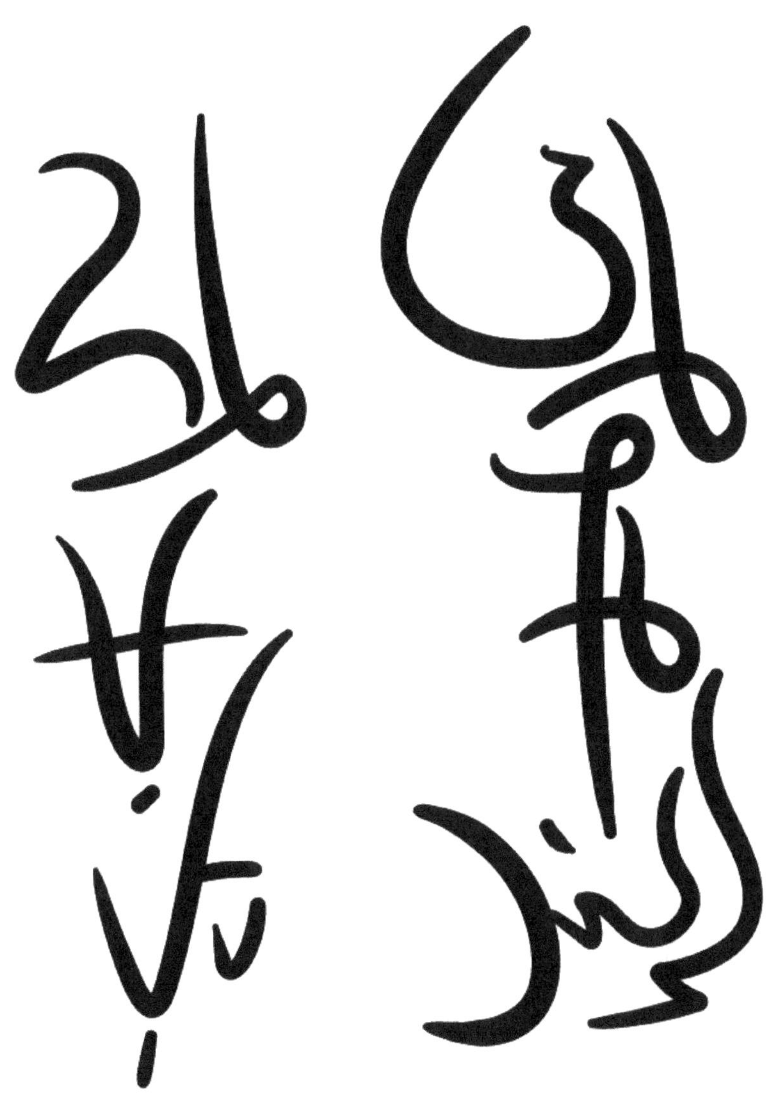

Sálángí Támu Pû

BÁYUNG PANAGÁNU
Foreword to the Second Edition

If you know how to write Kapampángan in its native script *Kulitan*, then you know Mike Pangilinan. Chances are that you learned from the master himself, as did many — if not most — of the artists and cultural advocates who have been giving, and are continuing ever more strongly to give, the native language of Indûng Kapampángan a distinctive and public face. If you don't know Kulitan yet, then this book will guide you there. It not only introduces the reader to Kulitan but takes you from zero Kulitan to reading proficiency through a thorough description and an abundance of illustrations from various domains of usage.

Beyond its practical mission of teaching Kulitan, this book also traces the history of its usage and form from pre-colonial and Spanish colonial times up to the present in a scholarly approach, also investigating its origins and relationships in the larger South-East Asian context. Kulitan was probably never commonly known by the general Kapampángan populace, also because its usage was fairly limited compared to today's omnipresence of writing. But Kulitan was on the edge of oblivion in the 20th century, surviving to Mike Pangilinan's generation only by a thread. What's more, the historical documentation of Kulitan is very sparse because of the (partly intended) perishable nature of traditional writing materials. Mike Pangilinan not only dug into archives to find rare specimens of historical Kulitan writing, but he also meticulously tracked down and documented whatever knowledge of it still survived into his time in an impressive effort for which no one else would have been more qualified, thanks also to his vast social network in Indûng Kapampángan.

Luckily, Kulitan is in a much better position now than it was at the turn of the millennium, and this is largely thanks to Mike Pangilinan's fervent activism, which sparked a cultural movement that has taken on its own momentum. This renaissance of Kulitan has accelerated since the publication of the first edition of this book. Kulitan has since grown beyond the grassroot underground setting of the Angeles art scene and tattoo studios; it is now increasingly observed in public spaces — on logos of schools, small businesses and malls, but also on clothing and street art. Kulitan has entered the digital world and climbed to the political stage, facing new challenges and becoming ever stronger. This and more is covered in the present long-awaited second edition.

With this book, you become part of this exciting cultural renaissance. It can only be hoped that the language that Kulitan represents, the *Amánung Sísuan* of the Kapampángan, will experience a similar renaissance. The current trend is alarming, with Tagalog and English ever more encroaching on Kapampángan families, sucking at its vitality both on the edges and in the very heartland of Indûng Kapampángan. May Kulitan, as a beacon of Kapampángan identity, pride and resilience, battle this downward trend to reinvigorate the Kapampángan language and culture. And may you be a part of this. *Lúid ya ing Indûng Kapampángan!*

Kevin Bätscher, Ph.D.
Department of Linguistics
University of Hawaii

PANAGÁNU
Foreword

An introduction to KULITAN, the indigenous Kapampángan script is a long due and much awaited book. Despite the recent revival of interest in pre-Hispanic Kapampángan script, i.e. Kulitan, there had been no definite reference providing scholars, cultural activists, students and all Kapampángans together, with an overview of its origin, orthography, syntax and grammar. This time is gone as Michael Raymon Táyag-Manalóto Pángilínan aka Siuálâ ding Meángûbié here offers a perfect introduction to anyone interested in reading or writing Kapampángan using the Kulitan script.

Siuálâ ding Meángûbié has been one the pioneer scholars and activists who fostered the revival of Kapampángan culture back in the 1990s. Over the last decade and a half he has accumulated considerable, probably unique, knowledge and skills with regards to the Kapampángan language and its cultural context. In his study of the Amánung Sísuan, Siuálâ ding Meángûbié has the immense merit of combining dominant Western approaches with South and East Asian academic and philosophical framings. He has further complemented academic scholarship with rigorously collected and verified local knowledge from all throughout Indûng Kapampángan. This puts him in the best position to write this authoritative introduction to the Kulitan script.

In this book, Siuálâ ding Meángûbié provides an articulated rationale for using Kulitan instead of the dominant, actually hegemonic, Latin script imposed by the Spanish conquistadors some 400 years ago. He notably draws upon a wide array of historical and linguistic materials to trace

25

the roots and structure of the Kulitan script. He eventually continues by providing the basic orthographic, syntax and grammatical rules using numerous illustrated examples which help the student in practicing and mastering Kulitan. The book closes with a glimpse of what the future of Kulitan may be in the context of the present movement for the revival of Kapampángan culture.

This volume is obviously informative, but its contributions go much beyond that. It provides a path breaking, precise, critical and challenging analysis of the place and role of the Kapampángan language and Kulitan script in contemporary society. It is neither a romanticised view of an ancient phenomenon nor a delusional or blind advocacy for a radical cultural agenda. It is a well-informed and impressive academic reference as well as a key text for laymen interested in understanding their cultural and historical roots and mastering their own language. In that sense, it paves the way for more scholarly studies in the field of linguistics, anthropology and history to advance our knowledge of the Kulitan script, and for a revival of its instruction in contemporary school and university curricula.

It is therefore much expected that this introductory book will be followed by a comprehensive syntax and grammar text book and eventually a work book for students of Kulitan to practice and improve their skills. Meanwhile I strongly recommend that everyone interested in the Kapampángan culture give a close read to this volume which will likely change our perception of the Amánung Sísuan.

Luid ya ing kulitan! Luid ya ing Kapampángan!

JC Gaillard

The University of Auckland

BÁYUNG TALUGÍGÎ
Preface to the Second Edition

It has been more than ten years since the publication of my book, *An Introduction to Kulitan, the indigenous Kapampángan script.* It was the first book ever written on the subject. Since then, interest in learning the script has increased and several workshops and seminars have been conducted in teaching it. A demand for the book has grown and sadly for the past eight years, the book has already been sold out and remained out of print. It is with this increasing demand by the Kapampángan people, most especially the youth, that merited the printing of this second edition.

In this edition, the *Pámaglábung* (epilogue) has been expanded to become the *Katlung Dangkâ* (Part III) of the book. Through the decade since the publication of the first edition, Kulitan has become more visible in several domains. More writers have come out and became active. New writers have been trained and are now training others. Still, Kulitan is far from being safe. Kulitan remains threatened as the Kapampángan language itself, more so since there are less writers vis-à-vis the number of speakers. A majority of Kapampángan speakers remain illiterate in it and even unaware of its existence. A lot still has to be done to keep Kulitan, like the Kapampángan language itself, from dying out.

Apart from the *Katlung Dangkâ* (Part III), additional chapters have also been inserted into the first two parts of the book. A number of chapters have also been modified. The new chapters include a discussion on Kapampángan numerals and a separate chapter on the reason why Kulitan does not need to invent a separate glyph for the /r/ sound.

As for modified chapters, the chapter *Báyung Súlî* (Innovations) was almost deleted since most Kulitan writers strongly rejected the proposed "new" glyphs as unnecessary. Instead of totally deleting it, it was modified instead. A couple of the proposed glyphs and writing innovations that are still under consideration were retained in the chapter. The proposed new glyphs to represent the /t͡ʃ/, /dʒ/ and / ʃ/ sounds were no longer included in this second edition since they were totally rejected and deemed unnecessary.

Robert La Rue, a native English speaker from Colorado (USA) and an active member of the Kapampángan art community in Angeles City, was gracious enough to proofread the entire first edition for free after its publication in case I needed to publish a second edition. Robert is one of the few Americans I know who seriously studied the Kapampángan language and is currently struggling with its native script, Kulitan.

Many of those who read the first edition have noticed the glaring typographical errors and grammatical inconsistencies throughout the book. The first edition was never edited nor proofread. The fault was entirely mine. I was pressed for time and did not have the resources to hire a proofreader and editor. As a constant victim of plagiarists and intellectual thievery, I did not trust anyone with the contents of the book. The manuscript was sent directly to the layout designer and then to the printer. Mistakes were inevitable there too. In the process, some of the texts went missing and a couple of *garlit* or 'dots' that alter the vowel sounds in the Kulitan text images were mistakenly erased as smudges in the process of cleaning and enhancing the images.

Sadly, I have committed the same mistake with this second edition. Pressed for time, I hope Robert can forgive me for not asking his help to proofread the new chapters that I have added. I hope the errors would be minimal and not too glaring this time.

The publication of this second edition was made possible through the untiring efforts and support of the members and volunteers of the Ágúman Sínúpan Singsing, Inc. (ASSI), a non-government organization that aims to document, research, and promote Kapampángan language, history and culture through lectures, workshops and multimedia publications, as well as drafting legislations for the protection and promotion of Kapampángan language and culture.

My deepest and sincerest gratitude goes to the Administrative Director of ASSI, Alegria Táyag-Lansang Cruz, known to all of us as Joy, for taking charge of the publication of this second edition, and to her daughter Soleil Cruz, for taking charge of the layout and editing. Thanks too to Aljon (Albert Jonah) Pángilínan-Mallari Medina, the resident Kulitan instructor of ASSI, for volunteering to redo the Kulitan texts and charts for this second edition. Many of those who have read the first edition would immediately see the difference in the writing and calligraphic style.

Justin Calmâ Lacson who has worked with ASSI on several projects as a graphic artist has volunteered to design the book cover.

Special thanks to my good friend and colleague Kevin Bätscher, ASSI's resident linguist and regular visiting lecturer and researcher, for his review and critique of the second edition and in writing the *Báyung Panagánu* (Forward to the Second Edition).

In the process of writing this book, I also extend my sincerest gratitude for the constant support and untiring assistance of ASSI's regular volunteers, students and supporters, especially Raphael Aguipo, Gabriel Gatbonton, Krist John Lalic, Christian Manaloto, Jayken Figueroa, Nigel Christopher Ayson, Dominique Juntado, Roderick Soriano, Anton Soriano, Marco Pio Cunanan, Luzvimindo David, Romuel David, Ian Manalo Salenga, Dodgie Aguinaldo, Cecile Yumul, Rey Maniago, Nancy Lagman Tremblay, Edwin Navarro Camaya, JC Gaillard, Jermal Tuazon, Angela Andres, Ruselo Bustos Garcia, Marlon Jon Maristela and Krizia Chu Tranquilino.

The timely donation of much needed equipment from the Bridges of Benevolent Initiatives Foundation, Inc. (BBIFI) under Cóng Bong (Irineo Alvaro), a staunch advocate of Kapampángan language and literature, have helped immensely in facilitating the writing and editing of this book. The donation was made possible through Cóng Ed (Edgardo Pamintuan), the former mayor of Angeles City and currently the Chairman of the Board of Directors of Clark Development Corporation (CDC). It was under the mayorship of Cóng Ed that

Kapampángan cultural heritage were revitalized and an ordinance to protect and promote the Kapampángan language in Angeles City was signed into law. Cóng Bong *at* Cóng Ed, *dakal a dakal pung salámat king pámagmasabal yu pû!*

I also have to extend my sincerest gratitude to other Kapampángan advocates who personally extended their assistance and support in the course of my writing this book, namely Maureen Gepte Castro and Mama Rey (Rey Yumang), former Kapampángan talk show hosts of GNN44's *Personalan*; Chan Alvarez, a visual artist and former provincial tourism officer of the province of Pampanga; and Norma Maita del Rosario of the political del Rosario clan of Ángeles City and her husband Edward Nucup. *Dakal pung salámat kékayu!*

Lastly, I would have to thank the people I constantly brainstormed with in the process of writing this book, to Nigel Christopher Ayson and Christian Mánalóto for the monthly intellectual discourse that helped stimulate a mind that would have stagnated due to my social isolation, and to Marco Luis Zapanta who visited me every weekend in the midst of my depression. The discussions, stories, rants, and endless discourse over masala chai, suklating batirul, and Kirin Ichiban Beer gave me the much-needed energy and strength to struggle with my depression and finish the writing of this book. *Laus lub kung pásalámat kékayu ngan!!! É kayu sána sásáwâ kanáku!!!*

To all the people I failed to mention, my wholehearted apologies and sincerest gratitude! *Dakal a dakal pung salámat karing sablang sáup yu! Luíd támu ngan pû!*

齋部雷衛門神威
Michael Raymon Táyag-Manalóto Pángilínan
Indung Kapampángan
2023 March 18

TALUGÍGÎ
Preface

The indigenous Kapampángan script or *Kulitan*, has always been a source of pride for the Kapampángan people, even if the majority of them cannot read and write in it. I learned *Kulitan* or *Súlat Kapampángan* when I was fourteen years old during my second year of high school. My sincerest gratitude goes to my maternal grandparents, the master story tellers Ápûng Éliung (Cornelio Manaloto y Toledano) and Ápûng Nénâ (Elena Tayag y Limcolioc [林高柳]), as well as to my grand aunts and grand uncles in the Tayag and Manaloto clans of Magalang where I grew up as a child. Magalang is a quiet little town in the foothills of Bunduk Aláya (Mount Arayat), at the heart of Indûng Kapampángan. Bunduk Aláya is the home of the Kapampángan sun god Ápûng Sínukuan. Many people in Magalang still believed in and venerated him back when I was growing up. Considered the father of Kapampángan civilization, Ápûng Sínukuan was said to have been the one who taught Kapampángans how to express their thoughts in written form. Being written top to bottom, right to left, kulitan is said to be a *pásingtábî* or homage to the movements of the sun. Refer to the following verse [Fig. 1]:

Anting Aldó síslag banua
Kéti súlip áslagan na.
Sisílang ya king Aláya,
King Pinatúbû lulbug ya.

Like the Sun that shines from heaven,
Its radiance reaches down on earth.
Rising from Bunduk Aláya,
It descends on Mount Pinatubo.

Figure 1. The Kapampángan verse that pays homage to the sun
and explains why Kulitan is written vertically from right to left
[Brushed by Raymond Bondoc Figueroa of San Luis, Pampanga.]

The first two lines refer to Kulitan being written vertically, top to bottom.
The rays of the sun spread down to earth from the heavens, hence top
to bottom. The last two lines refer to Kulitan being written right to left.
When facing the North Star or *Tálâng Úgut*, Bunduk Aláya on the East
sits on your right hand while Bunduk Pinatúbû on the West sits on your
left, thus explaining the writing direction from right to left.

As the Kapampángan god of war, the sun god Ápûng Sínukuan (Tagalog *Ápôlaki*) is also known as *Bayang* (白陽), the destroyer (*manlasak*). He is the white noonday sun that appeared on Katipunan flags and was worshipped by *bayánî* or warrior heroes. It was *Bayang* that the Spaniards emasculated and renamed Maria, i.e. Mariang Sinukuan, whose anger the Katipunan mystics sought to awaken during the revolution against Spain. The *Katipunan* or *Kataastaasang Kagalanggalangang Katipunan ng mga Anak ng Bayan* (KKK), the late 19th century revolutionary movement that sought to topple Spanish rule, was also a Kapampángan enterprise despite its Tagalog name. At that time, the word Tagalog was purely a geographic and non-ethnic term. It comes from the word *alug* or the flooded lowlands that surrounded *Lúsung* (Manila Bay), which of course include the province of Pampanga. The initial members of the Katipunan, including its founder Andres Bonifacio, were either pure blooded Kapampángan or Tagalog speakers of Kapampángan descent. The old Luzon capital of Tondo (東都), the birthplace of the Katipunan, was a Kapampángan enclave even before the coming of the Spaniards. In fact, Andres Bonifacio's Masonic name was Sínukuan, after the Kapampángan sun god, Ápûng Sínukuan.

According to *Akademyang Kapampángan* folklore, it was the Katipunan mystic and playwright Aurelio Tolentino of Wáwâ (偎岸) [Guagua], the old economic capital of the province of Pampanga, who sought to revive the cult of Ápûng Sínukuan and the pre-colonial civilization of the Kapampángan and Tagalog nations that included the writing systems of *Kulitan* and *Baybayin*. He was one of the initial members of the Katipunan and a good friend of its founder, Andres Bonifacio. A bilingual writer, Aurelio Tolentino is better known in Philippine History as the Father of Tagalog drama. It was the Katipunan who implemented Jose Rizal's proposal to indigenize Tagalog orthography in the Latin script based on the *Baybayin*. Aurelio Tolentino carried out the same thing for Kapampángan orthography based on his knowledge of the *Kulitan*. After Tolentino's death, Don Zoilo Hilario, a relative of Aurelio Tolentino by marriage, co-founded the Akademyang Kapampángan in 1937 with the leading writers of Wáwâ, namely Amado Yuzon and Monico Mercado, to continue the Katipunan's task of indigenizing Kapampángan orthography.

The cult of Ápûng Sínukuan and the practice of using the indigenous scripts to write talismans and commune with the ancestral spirits were said to be a part of the rituals of the various mystic cults that became popular among Kapampángan peasants in the 1880s, a decade or so before the founding of the Katipunan in Tondo in 1896. These cults were most prolific among the peasant communities that surrounded the *Pinak* (Candaba Swamp) and Bunduk Aláya (Mount Arayat). The Katipunan flag with the white noon day sun of Ápûng Sínukuan (Tagalog *Ápôlaki*) or Bayang (白陽) 'the destroyer superimposed with the indigenous script 'KA' (ᜃ) on the blood red background of Ápûng Maliári 'the life giver' is said to be a powerful talisman in Kapampángan mysticism. The Kapampángan revolutionary mystics who joined the ranks of the Katipunan might have injected some of their indigenous knowledge into the movement.

Like many of the scripts in Southeast Asia, the indigenous Kapampángan script has always been veiled in folklore, mysticism and taboos. For a long time, *Súlat Kapampángan* or *Kulitan* has been used by mystics and spiritual healers in their various rituals, especially in creating charms and talismans and in communicating with the ancestral spirits. Letters and petitions were written and burnt as a form of communication with the spirits of dead heroes and ancestors. Curses were also written in *Kulitan*, believing that they would acquire more potency if read and possessed or carried out by an ancestral spirit. A certain gravity and seriousness has therefore been attached to them, preventing the writer from trying to use them for communicating trivial mundane matters. One of the most enduring taboos in *Kulitan* is in using them to write foreign words or names. Another taboo is in teaching them to foreigners. It was for this reason that the majority of the Kapampángan people cannot read and write it despite the fact that the script has existed among them.

If the indigenous Kapampángan script is to survive in this present era, then it has to become a relevant means of expression among the living in this world, instead of it being used to communicate with the ancestral spirits in the next world.

In 1989, Edwin Navarro Camaya and I decided to do just that and began using *Kulitan* in our regular correspondence [Fig. 2]. I am sincerely grateful to Edwin for, if not for him, my knowledge in *Kulitan* would have gone to waste or simply been forgotten. Edwin was most enthusiastic in pushing for its revival and popularization in everyday communication. His brother, Emerson Navarro Camaya, was the first to encode the script in digital format and therefore make it possible to finally use and record them in computer word processing. A student of the University of the Philippines in Los Baños at that time, Edwin Camaya organized a group of Kapampángan students studying there in the mid-1990s and trained them to become cultural advocates and experts in *Kulitan*. For this I am indebted to one of my grand aunts from the Tayag-Lacson clan of Magalang, the late Ápûng Nénî (Evangelina Hilario Lacson), daughter of Don Zoilo Hilario and president emeritus of the Akademyang Kapampángan at that time. She was the one who pushed Edwin and me to become cultural warriors for Indûng Kapampángan. According to one of my grand uncles in Magalang, Ápûng Ambû (Paul Aquino), husband of my Ápûng Bidang (Brigida Manaloto) and a former commander of the Communist led Peoples Liberation Army Against Japan (HUKBALAHAP) and later The Peoples Liberation Army (HMB), Edwin is descended from a family of Kapampángan revolutionaries in the province of Tarlac.

Figure 2. A post card with notes written in Kulitan sent by Edwin Navarro Camaya to Michael Pangilinan in 1992, one of the many correspondences written in Kulitan.

Ápûng Ambû once mentioned that the indigenous scripts were revived during the Great Pacific War by a number of female couriers of the HUKBALAHAP from Candaba and Arayat who had undergone intelligence training under Squadron 48 in Bunduk Aláya. They were then called *Súlat Bayánî* or 'warriors' script" since they were identified with the revolutionary heroes of the Katipunan. Ápûng Ambû stressed that the struggle of the HUKBALAHAP, and later the HMB, were a continuation of the revolutionary struggles of the Katipunan.

The practice of using *Kulitan* and *Baybayin* in Huk communiqués was discontinued in 1943 when the scripts were identified with the *Kapisanan ng Paglilingkod sa Bagong Pilipinas* (KALIBAPI), a political party made up of intellectuals who supported the Japanese cause in Asia and used *Kulitan* and *Baybayin* in their display of nationalism. Although they have been demonized so much after the war, the KALIBAPI intellectuals and propagandists, like the Katipunan revolutionaries, sought to revive pre-colonial knowledge in order to create a new country devoid of any traces of Western colonialism. When Japan defeated Russia in 1905, she became a beacon of light for many Asian nations still languishing in the darkness of Western imperialism. The veterans of the revolution against Spain and the war against the United States saw Japan as Asia's saviour from white colonial rule. Rabidly anti-American, many of them and their descendants joined the KALIBAPI and supported Japan's war against the white colonialists in Asia. Sadly, Kapampángan nationalists became caught up in the politics of the foreign ideologies. One group joined the Communists. Another group joined the Fascists. The KALIBAPI was headed by Ápûng Ambû's cousin, Benigno Aquino, Sr., the father of Philippine hero Ninoy (Benigno Aquino, Jr.) and grandfather of the current Philippine president Noynoy (Benigno Aquino III).

I am also indebted to the late poet laureate from Magalang, Ápûng Viding (Vedasto Ocampo), who together with Kapampángan poet laureate Jose M. Gallardo of Candaba, was also said to have fought the Japanese in the resistance movement in the last Great Pacific War. He was at first apprehensive in reviving *Kulitan* because they were identified with the group of anti-American intellectuals who supported the Japanese cause in Asia, the KALIBAPI. Among the leading members of the KALIBAPI in Pampanga was none other than Don Zoilo Hilario, the founder and head of the Akademyang Kapampángan at that time. Despite that, Ápûng

Viding became the vice president of the Akademyang Kapampángan and the editor in chief of their quarterly publication, *Ing Susi*. He later agreed that the Kulitan belonged to the Kapampángan people and should not be identified, nor tied to, a particular group or individual. Under Josefina Dizon Henson's presidency, the Akademyang Kapampángan published my primer entitled *Pamagkulit King Kekatamung Matuang Kasulatan* in *Ing Susi* in 1995 [Fig. 3]. *Atching Josie* (Josefina Dizon Henson) with whom I am also grateful to is also well versed in *Kulitan*. She designed a new logo for the Akademyang Kapampángan with the use of the indigenous Kapampángan script.

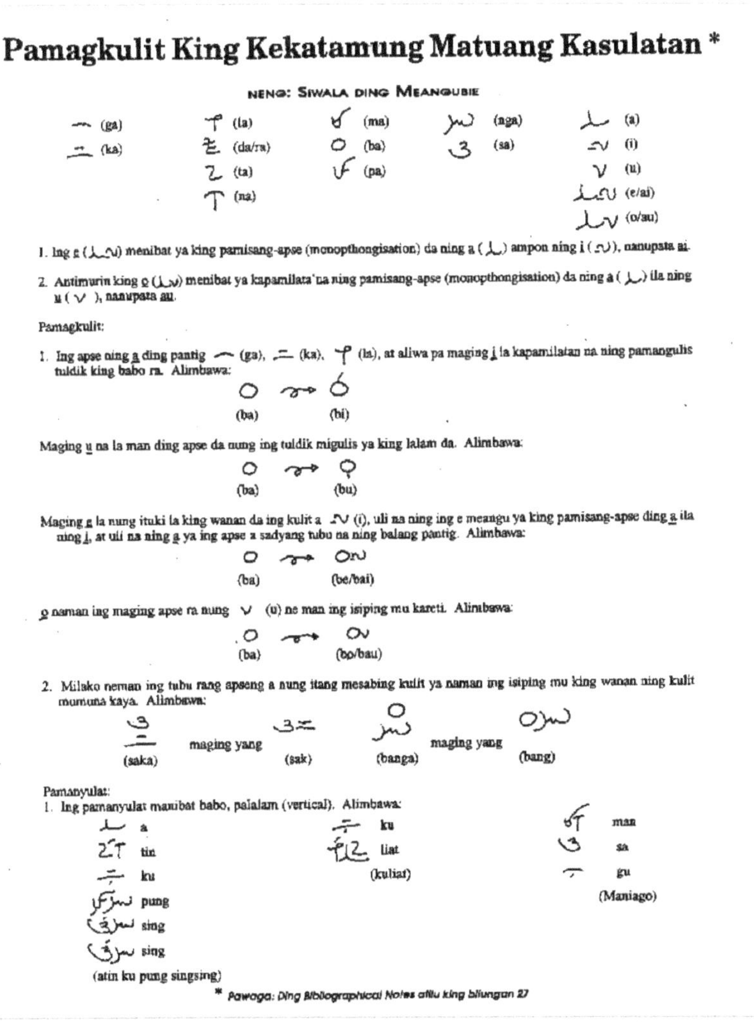

Figure 3. The Akademyang Kapampángan's Kulitan primer entitled Pamagkulit king Kekatamung Matuang Kasulatan published in their quarterly journal Ing Susi. It was originally written in 1989 by Siuálâ ding Meángûbié.

After the eruption of Mount Pinatubo in 1991, the Pampanga Arts Guild became my cultural and intellectual sanctuary in the then culturally deprived wasteland of Angeles City. My ideas and research in Kapampángan language and culture, including *Kulitan* or *Súlat Kapampángan*, found fertile ground in the creative minds of the local artists. I extend my sincerest thanks to Dan Táyag and Minerva Arceo who always helped organize the lecture workshops and exhibits; To Ronnie Táyag, Lorina Tayag Capitulo, Norman Tiotuico, Bruno Tiotuico, Gelo Espiritu, Paks Pineda and Edille Paras who were among the first to use the *Kulitan* in their various creative expressions [Fig. 4 & 5]; To Ysaganî Yátu Ybarra   (Marcelino Sigfried Ranada y Tiglao) and Cecil Yumul who always dream dreams and conceive concepts; To Badet Tiotuico, Nimo Tiotuico, Long Melo and the late Góriû (Gerry Bautista) who always attended my lectures and worked hard to learn Kulitan; To Allan David, Paul del Mundo, Jun Bap Cruz, Dennis Borja Meneses, Ruston Banal, Rafael Maniago, Robert Odejar, Benjie Ranada and my uncle Conderlos Lingat who always supported my advocacies, *Dakal a salámat*.

Figure 4. A watercolor painting by Ronnie Táyag with Kulitan script written horizontally.

Figure 5. A mixed-media art work by Gelo Espiritu with Biblical texts written in Kulitan.

When the internal politics of the Akademyang Kapampángan became too complicated and unbearable in the mid-1990s, Edwin Camaya and I left it to establish the Batiáuan Foundation together with Dave Nepomuceno in 1997. The goal of which was to popularize Kapampángan language and culture. This included the teaching of *Kulitan* in our various advocacy seminars and discussion programs. Those who were most active and highly supportive in the movement included Marco Nepomuceno and Abraham Táyag of Angeles City, Armando Regala, Manolo Gatbonton of Candaba and Nancy Lagman Tremblay of Minalin. To them, I am truly grateful.The efforts of Kragi Garcia, a multitalented artist from Macabebe, must also be noted and commended. Since the late 1990s, Kragi remains the only Kapampángan cultural advocate in the Kapampángan Delta Region. He has managed to maintain a small community of *Kulitan* writers in the coastal community of Batungdalig in the municipality of Masantol. According to folklore, Batungdalig was the birthplace of the warrior ruler Radjah Suliman who resisted the

43

Spaniards at the battle of Bangkusay in 1571. Batungdalig therefore is one of those rare Kapampángan communities that are extremely proud of their history and heritage. Of course, one cannot thank Kragi Garcia, without thanking Marcelo Bajun Lacap, Jr., the charismatic community leader of Batungdalig who constantly struggles to preserve their people's history and heritage.

In 1999, I was absorbed into Holy Angel University through the efforts of Marco Nepomuceno and Arlyn Sicangco Villanueva to develop a curriculum for the teaching of Kapampángan language and culture and the establishment of a centre for Kapampángan research. *Kulitan* literacy was an important part in teaching Kapampángan culture. Arlyn Sicangco Villanueva and Jess Panlilio were very supportive of my efforts and ideas in injecting Kapampángan culture into the College of Business and Accountancy. Very soon my efforts and ideas in creating a pro-Kapampángan curriculum were also supported by the College of Arts and Sciences, namely by the former Deans Rolando Diamante and Averell Laquindanum, as well as my fellow teachers Joel Regala, Joel Mallari, Lisa Cusi Simon, Narciso de Jesus, Fr. Enrique Luzung and the late Fr. Bonifacio Guanlao. It was at Holy Angel University where I met JC Gaillard from Grenoble, France who became a serious researcher in Kapampángan geography and culture and currently one of the non-ethnic Kapampángans who can read and write *Kulitan*.

In the year 2001, the Center for Kapampángan Studies was established through the joint efforts of the Batiáuan Foundation, spearheaded by Marco Nepomuceno and myself, and Holy Angel University, represented by Vice President for Student Affairs Robby Tantingco, CBA Dean Arlyn Villanueva Sicangco and Chief Librarian Nimfa Maniago. The indigenous Kapampángan script became an indispensable part of the Center, especially through the efforts of Joel Mallari and Arnel Garcia who kept *Kulitan* alive in their various publications and creative expressions.

Another Kapampángan cultural advocate worth commending is John Manuntag, a young architect from the marshland region of Candaba. John is one of the first to use *Kulitan* in digital art and advertising and is actively pushing for its use among popular commercial icons [Fig. 6 & 7].

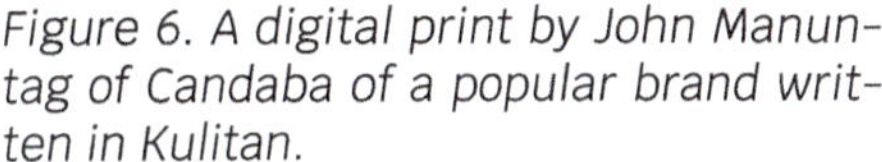

Figure 6. A digital print by John Manuntag of Candaba of a popular brand written in Kulitan.

Figure 7. A digital print by John Manuntag of Candaba of a popular brand written in Kulitan.

Perhaps there is no single person that has made *Kulitan* admired by Kapampángans at home and abroad in the past five years more than Marlon Jon Castro Maristela. Marlon is a young Kapampángan tattoo artist from Angeles City, a native of Bamban in the province of Tarlac, and a member of the mystic commune of Baliti on the slopes of Bunduk Aláya. His *Batik Kulitan* or *Kulitan* tattoos made quite an impact on a growing number of Kapampángan youths who proudly wear them as a testament of their pride in their ethnic Kapampángan identity [Fig. 8]. Marlon's skills and advocacy to promote Kapampángan culture deserve our praise and recognition. Of course, this would not be complete without our mutual friend, my late nephew, Kit Táyag, who was the first person to step in and have his body tattooed in *Kulitan* [Fig. 9]. Kit was a very charismatic young artist who is extremely proud and expressive of his ethnic Kapampángan identity. He is quite influential among his peers who would have ended up as foreigners in their own native land if not for him. To Kit, I extend my constant prayers and gratitude.

Figure 8. A Batik Kulitan (Kulitan Tattoo) by Marlon Jon Castro Maristela on Kapampángan-American Jill Pangilinan de Leon.

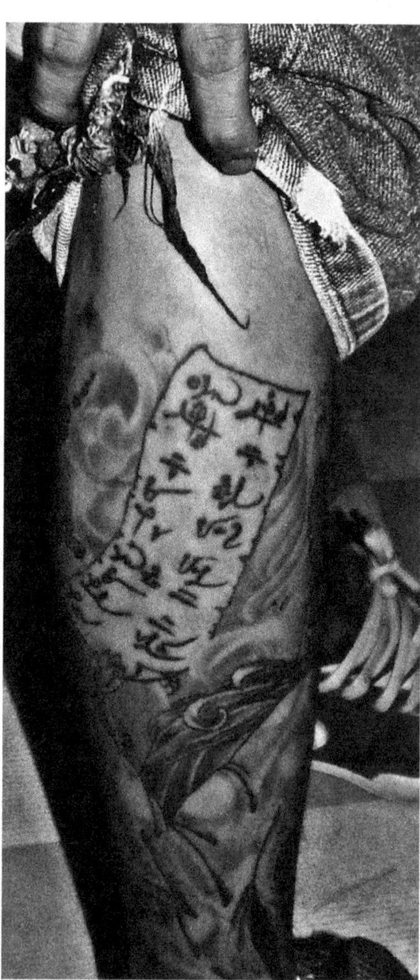

Figure 9. The first ever Batik Kulitan (Kulitan Tattoo) by Marlon Jon Castro Maristela on Kit Tayag.

When Ápûng Ambô (Rev. Fr. Virgilio Pablo David) was ordained a bishop in 2006, he incorporated the indigenous Kapampángan script in his coat of arms, perhaps the first minister of the Roman Catholic Church to ever do so [Fig. 10]. His move is very symbolic and highly significant for Kapampángan culture. To him I extend my deepest respect and gratitude.

Figure 10. The coat of arms of Ápûng Ambû (Rev. Fr. Virgilio Pablo S. David), Auxilliary Bishop of San Fernando, Pampanga, with word Aláya written in Kulitan.

In 2008, the *Ágúman Súlat Kapampángan* was organized through the untiring efforts of Eliver Tanhueco Sicat, Mark Ebbol Rosales, John Balatbat (林銀龍) and Bruno Tiotuico. The goal of the organization is to gather everyone who can read and write *Kulitan* and create a school to teach it to the general Kapampángan public. This is in response to a number of *Kulitan* writers who are content to be literate in it but are unwilling to share their knowledge to a greater number of people. The *Ágúman* managed to recruit among their ranks the young Kulitan writers Diego Dobles (鄺杰功) of Angeles City, John Manuntag of Candaba and Marcelo Lacap III and Michael Cabrera of the proud Kapampángan village of Batungdalig in Masantol, Lucio Sison of the Museo ning Angeles and and Ronnie Táyag of the Pampanga Arts Guild. I hope my praise and gratitude will not be an added burden for this hard working group [Fig. 11 & 12].

In 2009, *Kulitan* became the subject of the paper I presented at the 11th International Conference on Austronesian Linguistics (11ICAL) at Aussois, France. Entitled *Assessing the current status of the Kapampángan "pre-Hispanic" script*, it was the first time that the indigenous Kapampángan script was formally introduced to the international academic community. It became available to the rest of the world when it was published online at the 11ICAL website. My heartfelt gratitude goes to the organizers of the 11ICAL and the scientific and cultural attaché of the Embassy of France in Manila, namely Marie Aurousseau, Isabelle Eppaillard and Flora Gelley, who became faithful supporters of Kapampángan culture and the indigenous Kapampángan script.

Soon after the publication of my 11ICAL paper on the internet, a number of Kapampángans who could read and write *Kulitan* have stepped forward to help support the movement that is keeping it alive. Many of them are currently based outside of the archipelago. Exposed to other non-Latin scripts around the globe, they have developed their own style and convention in writing the indigenous Kapampángan script. These include Japan-based Mervin Manangan, Alfred Íbé Malazza and Chiles Jersey Dizon; Mark Ian Carlos Cortez in the Middle East; and Manolito Dizon in Australia. John Manuntag of Candaba was also based for a time in the Middle East. Many of them have overcome the existing taboos that still have a grip on many *Kulitan* writers based in *Indúng*

Figure 11. The Ágúman Súlat Kapampángan drapes the Museo ning Angeles with Kulitan banners.

Figure 12. A Kulitan art exhibit by Ágúman Súlat Kapampángan at the Pamintuan ancestral mansion in Angeles City in February 2012.

Kapampángan and are quite vocal in proposing innovations to make the script relevant to the general public.

Perhaps the most interesting individual among *Kulitan* writers outside *Indûng Kapampángan* is Yavre Canda Nupsa who has quite a following among *Baybayin* advocates abroad. A Kapampángan-American who learned *Súlat Kapampángan* outside of Indûng Kapampángan, Yavre did not grow up writing *Kulitan* with any of the taboos and conventions that have been traditionally attached to it. His occasional clash with the traditional *Kulitan* writers online is quite understandable and refreshing to a point. I am extremely grateful for his undying effort to promote the script of our ancestors to an international community exposed only to the Tagalog *Baybayin*. His instructional video that is currently uploaded on youtube is by far the most entertaining and easy to understand *Kulitan* primer to date.

Thanks to the power of the internet, a growing number of non-Kapampángans began to study the indigenous Kapampángan script and have become actively supportive in teaching it and keeping it alive. Among the most dynamic are Nordenx (Norman de los Santos), a Filipino-American with roots in Mindoro, and Akopito Ardinez, a Dublin-based native of Mindanao. These two deserve every praise and gratitude from the Kapampángan people.

In the 2010 article *Galit sa Kulit* that he wrote in his blog *Baybayin Modern Fonts* [*Anak Bathala Project*], Nordenx explains the uniqueness of *Súlat Kapampángan* to an international audience, particularly the Filipino-American community who were initially exposed only to the traditional Tagalog *Baybayin*.

His article was the most concise and easy to understand overview of *Kulitan* ever written. In the same blog, Nordenx prepared a *cuaderno* of all the existing *Kulitan* abecedaries from 1699 to 2008, as well as designed a downloadable true type font for digital encoding. He is currently active in the discussion group created by the *Águman Súlat Kapampángan* on Facebook where he generously shares his knowledge and insight on *Kulitan*.

Apart from devoting pages to his native *Suwat Bisaya*, the Dublin-based native of Mindanao Akopito Ardinez dedicated a very detailed page on the teaching of the indigenous Kapampángan script in his personal website. The page is complete with an abecedary, a video link and detailed instructional charts and diagrams for those willing to learn it. Some of the charts and diagrams found in this book were inspired directly from Akopito's page. In addition to his page on *Súlat Kapampángan*, in his website, Akopito also created a video demonstrating the Kapampángan way of writing. A quiet person, Akopito deserves the praise and gratitude of the Kapampángan people in helping to teach and save their indigenous heritage.

Among the non-Kapampángan members of the academe who deserve my eternal gratitude in showing a particular interest in the study of the indigenous Kapampángan script are JC Gaillard from France, Zeus Salazar from the University of the Philippines and Christopher Ray Miller from Canada. Zeus Salazar, who established the school of thought *Pantayong Pananaw* and heads the *Bahay Saliksikan ng Kasaysayan ~ Bagong Kasaysayan* (BAKAS), Inc., announced that he has seen the beginnings of Philippine indigenous calligraphy in *Súlat Kapampángan* and was gracious enough to name me the *Ama ng Kaligrapiyang Pilipino* or "Father of Filipino Calligraphy".

The person that I could never thank enough in writing this book is Christopher Ray Miller. His research on Southeast Asian scripts, including *Baybayin* and *Súlat Kapampángan*, has helped push further the scholarship on the indigenous scripts of the archipelago. His works, both published and unpublished, are cited in practically every chapter of this book, including the images on 16th to 17th century Kapampángan signatures that are a product of his untiring search into every archive around the globe. These he generously shared with me and without cost, which I now also share in this book for the benefit of the general Kapampángan public. A lifetime of "thank you" would not be enough to repay Chrisopher Ray Miller for his constant effort in furthering the study of the indigenous Kapampángan script.

I would like to thank in earnest all those who helped to make this book possible. First of all, I would like to thank the Center for Kapampángan Studies at Holy Angel University who painstakingly worked on editing and publishing my book, especially to Leonardo Calma who did an excellent work in doing the overall layout and design, to Myra Paz Lopez who handled all the necessary papers and requirements, and of course to the director, Robby Tantingco, who, despite the countless headaches and stress I have given him in the past decade, has kept his faith in my efforts and ideas for the development of Kapampángan studies. It was his efforts that pushed me to finally write this long overdue book on *Kulitan*. I also extend my thanks to the friends and consultants of the Center, Professor Lino Dizon, Alex Castro and Erli Mendoza, who in one way or another may have helped influence the writing of this book.

I am also very much indebted to all my friends and acquaintances in the international academic community. First of all I would like to thank my mentors and friends from whom I learned my little knowledge of Kapampángan linguistics, Dr. Anicia del Corro of the Philippine Bible Society and Kitano Hiroaki from the Aichi University of Education in Nagoya, Japan. I am also grateful to my friends from the international Austronesian linguistics community who always generously shared their knowledge and ideas during our various exchanges, especially to Elisabeth Luquin, John Wolff, Steve Quakenbush, David Gil, Imanishi Kazuhiro, Nojima Motoyasu, Nagai Naonori, Katagiri Masumi, Osumi Midori, Aone van Engelenhoven, Waruno Mahdi, Tom Hoogervorst, Liao Hsiuchuan, Li Taiyuan and Mike Tanankinsing.

I would also like to thank my mentors and colleagues at the University of the Philippines Archaeological Studies Program (UP-ASP), especially to my professors Dr. Eusebio Dizon of the National Museum who trusted me so much with my knowledge and research into the indigenous

Siuálâ ding Meángûbié
Michael Raymon Táyag-Manalóto Pángilínan
齋部靈衛門神威

PAUAGA
Prologue

It is probably safe to say that the Philippines today is a state whose citizens are confused about their identity, ignorant of their history and unmindful of their heritage. Despite the advancement of archaeology and scholarly research into her pre-colonial past, the average student still learns in class that Philippine history began only with the coming of the Europeans in the early 16th century. This implies that the people of these islands would never have become part of the "civilized world" had it not been "discovered" by Western adventurers, namely by the Portuguese explorer Fernão de Magalhães who 'discovered' these islands for Spain in 1521. It is no surprise then why the average citizen of these islands proudly wears the brand of a 16th century foreign monarch in whose name his ancestors were tyrannized and his country raped and plundered for more than three hundred years. *Philippines* and *Filipino* are alien words that hold no indigenous significance in any of the ethnic languages of the archipelago. They are names derived from Philip II, the 16th century Spanish king.

These non-native names, Philippines and Filipino, have for generations now been used to promote a new form of colonialism among the indigenous inhabitants of this archipelago (Martinez, 2004; DILA, 2007). By law, the term Filipino now stands for the nationality, citizenship and national language of all the ethnolinguistic groups within these islands (Constitution of the Republic of the Philippines, 1987). Since then, all the indigenous languages and cultures of the various ethnolinguistic groups within the archipelago have been politically reduced to the status of mere "regional dialects." They are now being sacrificed and pushed to the brink of extinction in the name of a contrived "national" unity. To be Filipino is to speak Filipino, which is actually just another form of the Tagalog language in a clever disguise. In reality, Filipino nationalism is just an alternative word for Manila-Tagalog Imperialism. National unity is a convenient excuse for a new form of non-violent ethnic cleansing (Mantawe, 1998; Avila, 2007; DILA, 2007 and Dacudao, pers. comm., 2012 April 13-15). How Tagalog became synonymous with Filipino is discussed in detail in the community website of the Save Our Languages Through Federalism Foundation, Inc. (SOLFED) and Defenders of the Indigenous Languages of the Archipelago (DILA), and in the book *Filipino is NOT Our Language*, published by DILA in 2007.

Long before the idea of a Filipino nation was even conceived, the Kapampángan, Butuanon, Tausug, Magindanau, Hiligaynon, Sugbuanon, Waray, Iloko, Sambal and many other ethnolinguistic groups within the archipelago, already existed as *bangsâ* or nations in their own right. Many of these nations formed their own states and principalities centuries before the Spaniards created the Philippines in the late 16th century. The oldest of these states include Butuan (蒲端), which existed in Chinese records as early as 1001 C.E., Sulu (蘇祿), in 1368 C.E., and the Kingdom of Luzon (呂宋国), in 1373 C.E. These three sovereign states were ruled by kings (國王) and not by chieftains, according to Chinese historical records (Zhang, 1617; Scott 1989; Wang 1989; Wade, 2005 and Wang, 2008).

The Kapampángan nation was once a part of the Kingdom of Luzon [Fig. 13]. Kapampángans were one of the *Luçoes*, "people of Luzon," encountered by Portuguese explorers during their initial ventures into Southeast Asia in the early 16th century (Scott, 1994). The Kapampángan homeland, *Indûng Kapampángan* (Pampanga), became the first province carved out of the Kingdom of Luzon when the Spaniards conquered it in 1571 C.E. (Cavada, 1876 and Henson, 1965). Indûng Kapampángan's political boundaries once encompassed a large portion of the central plains of Luzon, stretching from the eastern coastline of the Bataan Peninsula in the Southwest, all the way to Casiguran Bay in the Northeast (Murillo Velarde, 1744; San Antonio, 1744; Beyer, 1918; Henson, 1965; Larkin, 1972 and Tayag, 1985) [Fig 14.]. It was said to be the most populated region in Luzon at that time, with an established agricultural base that could support a huge population (Loarca, 1583; San Agustin,

Figure 13. The Kingdom of Luzon (呂宋國) as it appears on a Japanese map during the Ming dynasty (1368 to 1644). From "A look at history based on Ming dynasty maps" (從大明坤輿萬國圖看歷史) posted by zhaijia1987 in Baidu Tieba (百度贴吧) on 2010 November 11.

Figure 14. Map of Pampanga from Pedro Murillo Velarde's 1744 *Mapa de las Islas Filipinas.* The Pampanga Delta Region had been inaccurately assigned to Bulacan.

1699; Mallat, 1846; B&R, 1905; Henson, 1965 and Larkin, 1972).

It also had a highly advanced material culture where Chinese porcelain was used extensively, and where firearms and bronze cannons were manufactured (Morga, 1609; Mas, 1843; B&R, 1905; Beyer, 1947; Larkin, 1972; Santiago, 1990b and Dizon, 1999). The old capital of the Kingdom of Luzon, Tondo (東都: "Eastern Capital"), once spoke one language with the rest of Indûng Kapampángan that was different from the language spoken in Manila (Loarca, 1583; B&R, 1905 and Tayag, 1985). Jose Villa Panganiban, the former commissioner of the Institute of National Language, once thought the Pasig River that divides Tondo and Manila to be the actual dividing line between Kapampángan and Tagalog (Tayag, 1985). The descendants of the old rulers of the Kingdom of Luzon, namely those of Salalílâ, Lakandúlâ and Suliman, can still be found all over Indûng Kapampángan (Beyer, 1918; Beyer, 1943; Henson, 1965 and Santiago, 1990a).

If the Kapampángan nation made up the bulk of the population of the Kingdom of Luzon, then perhaps the oldest evidence of Kapampángan writing can be found in the jars (呂宋壺) exported to Japan prior to the arrival of the Spaniards in the 16th century C.E. [Fig. 15]. In his book *Tokiko* (陶器考) or "Investigations of Pottery" published in 1853 C.E., Tauchi Yonesaburo (田内米三郎) presents several jars marked with the *ruson koku ji* (呂宋國字) or the "writing of the Kingdom of Luzon" (Tauchi [田内], 1853 and Cole, 1912). The marks that looked like the Chinese character *ting* (丁) found in several Luzon jars might have been the indigenous Kapampángan script *la* (ᜎ), the first syllable in the name "Luzon" [Fig. 16].

Writing has always been a testament to civilization among the great nations. The Chinese write "civilization" as *wénmíng* (文明) or "enlightenment through writing," combining the characters *wén* (文) "writing" and *míng* (明) "rightness." Sadly, the Kapampángan nation, a once proud civilization with a long established literature has now become a tribe of confused barbarians. Although many Kapampángans can read and write fluently in foreign languages, namely Filipino and English, they are strangely illiterate in their own native Kapampángan language.

57

Figure 15. A typical brown-glazed four-eared Luzon jar (呂宋壺〔褐釉四耳壺〕) *exported to Japan by the Kingdom of Luzon in the mid-16th century. Photo courtesy of Hikone Castle Museum* (彦根城博物館) *Newsletter, Vol. 13, 1991 May 1.*

of a tripod vessel (*gotoku*) with which it is provided is also a tripod vessel of the Namban.

On the preceding pages the difference between Korean and Namban pottery has been explained. Further details will follow. Namban are the various countries as described in the previous notes (*koguchi-gaki*).

Namban pottery provided with the seal of the oven from which it originates is usually not recognized as such by our contemporaries, though clay and glaze point to its being Namban. The mark ⊤ [1] finely made on Imbe ware, the mark ✕ on a jar (*tsubo*) of Bizen, the mark ⊥ three times on a tea-canister (*cha-ire*) of the same ware, and the mark Roku-zō on a pitcher (*mizusashi*), and marks on several other potteries represent the national writing of Luzon (*Luzon-no kokuji*).[2] Also a deep-brown glazed tea-canister (*shibu yaku-no cha-ire*) on which the character ⊥ [3] is written consists of Namban clay. Some of these marks may have been produced by Japanese who crossed over; but others may have been made by the natives (*Man-jin*), for it cannot be ruled that Namban has no marks of the furnace. There is, *e. g.*, on a fire-pan (*hi-ire*) of Annam the mark *Ta-kang* [4] impressed by means of a seal, which is the name of the maker. The tea-canisters called Chōsen-Garatsu (Korean Karatsu) [5] which have a plant-green (*moyegi*) glaze and purplish clay, or also dark-brown (*shibu*) glaze with purplish clay are taken by our contemporaries for real Karatsu-make on account of their seals of the furnace, but I consider them as foreign manufac-

[1] This is a Chinese character (*ting*, Jap. *tei*). Imbe pottery is characterized by a great variety of peculiar marks the significance of most of which is unknown (see MORSE, pp. 49 *et seq.*).

[2] The following characters, found in Philippine alphabets, resemble somewhat the markings on these vessels: ⊤ Pampanga; ⱬ Tagalog; ⱬ Ilocano, equivalents for *la;* ⱬ Visayan; ⊤ Pampanga and Tagbanua for *na;* ✕ Tagbanua for *ka.* [F. C. C.]

[3] Denoting the numeral 7.;
[4] The two characters are transcribed according to the Annamite pronunciation.
[5] BRINKLEY, p. 310.

Figure 16. A page in Faye–Cooper Cole's English translation of Tauchi Yonesaburo's Tokiko (陶器考) showing the 'national writing of Luzon' (呂宋國字) in comparison to Philippine scripts.

The Kapampángan language currently does not possess a standard written orthography. The dispute over which orthography to use when writing the Kapampángan language in the Latin Script ~ whether to retain the old Spanish style orthography a.k.a. Súlat Bacúlud, or implement the indigenized Súlat Wáwâ which replaced the Q and C with the letter K, remains unsettled. This unending battle on orthography has taken its toll on the development of Kapampángan literature and the literacy of the Kapampángan speaking majority (Pangilinan, 2006 and 2009b). No written masterpiece that could rival the works of the Kapampángan literary giants of the late 19th and early 20th centuries has yet been written. The few poems that earned a number of contemporary poets the title of Poet Laureate, no longer have the same impact that would immortalize them in the people's collective memory. Worse, the Kapampángan language is now even showing signs of decay and endangerment (Del Corro, 2000 and Pangilinan, 2009b).

While the old literary elite continue to bicker endlessly over which Latinized attitudinal procedure to follow, a small, yet growing number of Kapampángan youth have become frustrated and disillusioned with the current state of Kapampángan language and culture. They see the old Spanish style orthography, that still uses the letters C & Q, as a perpetuation of Spain's hold on the intellectual expressions of the Kapampángan people. The new orthography that has replaced the letters C and Q with K is also viewed to be foreign since they identify it with the Tagalog abakada. Instead of being forced to choose which orthography to use in writing Kapampángan, they chose to forego the use of the Latin script altogether. They decided instead to go back to writing in the indigenous *Súlat Kapampángan* or *Kulitan*.

PÁMALAGIÛ
Nomenclature

Fray Alvaro de Benavente (1699) and Fray Diego Bergaño (1732) wrote in their *Arte* and *Vocabulario* that the Kapampángan nation referred to the characters used in their indigenous scripts as *culit* [Fig. 17]. Utilizing his proposed indigenized Latin orthography that replaces the letters C & Q with the letter K, Don Zoilo Hilario (1962) naturally wrote *culit* as *kulit* in referring to these same characters. The whole writing system is therefore logically termed *Kulitan* according to Siuálâ ding Meángûbié, Edwin Camáya and Marco Nepomuceno of the Batiáuan Foundation, a Kapampángan research and advocacy group that popularized the use of the Kapampángan indigenous script through a series of lectures and publications in the late 1990s (Pangilinan, 2009a). The average Kapampángan however simply called the indigenous writing system as *Súlat Kapampángan* in contrast to the Latin and other foreign scripts. Kulitan and Súlat Kapampángan are therefore terms that are interchangeably used in reference to the indigenous Kapampángan script.

For a long time Kulitan was called *Alfabétong Kapampángan* or Kapampángan Alphabets by a number of scholars (Henson, 1965). The indigenous writings of these islands were once thought to be alphabets by many of those who tried to record or study them (Marche, 1887 and Marcilla, 1895). Years later, scholars who were exposed to other forms of writing other than the alphabets began classifying them as syllabaries (Henson, 1965). However, Kulitan, like many other Indian-inspired scripts in Asia and Southeast Asia, is not just a syllabary but an alphasyllabary or *abugida* (Pangilinan, 2009a). In an abugida,

que á uno le viene, ó por naturaleza,
por herencia. *Caliculi*, diminutivo es
cuando se le conoce muy poco lo que le
vino de herencia, v. g. si al Vizcaino,
ó Gallego, que ha aprendido con per-
feccion la lengua castellana se descuida,
ó desliza rarísima vez, que apenas se le
conoce, dirán: *Caliculimorin iny pañga
Gallegona. Mañguli, mengali*, es aquel en
quien se halla in acto secundo, lo que le
viene de atrás: atiende á los ejemplos, v. g.
el negro que se crió desde chico en Pa-
lacio como español, y luego le dió el
Sumpong, de volverse al monte: *Quinuli
ing pañga pugut na*. Cada instante lo
dicen de los que criados entre pampangos, y enseñados á comer en el *Dulang*,
macabular, se ván á comer sin mas mesa
que la olla, *Quinuli ing pañgapuguida*,
porque los negros comen asi. Á este modo,
si el abuelo fué brujo, y el padre no,
pero el nieto sí, dicen. *Quinuli itang pu-
hna:* lo mismo es en enfermedades, buen,
ó mâl proceder. *Pañgulian, peñgalian*, lo
que le viene de casta, &. Vide *Golo*.

CULILING. (pp.) N. S. El cordel del *Gaud*.

CULIMLIM. (pp.) Adjet. Cosa parda, mal
teñida, y lo dicen del que le pardea el
rostro, por tener algo de indio, y no sale
bien lo que tiene de español: *Culimlim*,
los llaman átomos del sol. *Ma*, N. pararse
dos colores en competencia: prot. el que
tiñe, y el que mira los átomos del sol,
porque se le turba la vista. Itt. El verbo.
N. de *Ma*, se dice de la honra, vir-
tud, &. que separa obscurecida, ó tur-
bia por algun descuido, ó vicio.

CULIPAT. (pp.) N. S. Ave de rapiña, rojo.

CULIPATPÁT. (pp.) Compuesto de *Lipatpát*.
V. N. se dice de las lucernas, cuando
están de monton en los árboles: abriendo,
y cerrando las alas.

CULIS. (a.) N. S. Árbol, con que tiñen
de amarillo el ebos.

CULISAC. (pp.) Syn. de *Acclis*.

CULISAP. (pp.) Piojo mayor que *Cumad*.

CULIT. (a.) N. S. Los puntillos de la es-
critura pampanga. *Mag*, aprender á leer
sus caracteres. 3. *Pagculitan*, la cartilla.

CULIT. (pp.) N. S. Dificultades, rodeos.
V. act. y su prot. Poner dificultades por
rodeos, v. g. El escribano cuando no
quiere despachar al pleiteante, y le dice
que no tiene alli los autos, que no está
alli el escribiente, &. Y tambien las dificultades, que ponen los que no quieren
echar la manceba, ó dejar la mala vida,

&. Y tambien el que anda por rodeos
jugando de los términos, siendo asi, que
lo entiende, v. g. Pido agua para beber,
y me responde: pide usted agua rosada?
agua de canela, agua de olor? P. 1. El
tratado asi, y tambien lo que se tuerce,
ó trae por rodeos, *ut* la peticion del agua
de beber, &. Mi, T. Mi, P. Mi, F. *Pi-
culitculitnaco. Ma*, de abundancia. *Tauo
yang maculit*, se dice bien de los que
son moledores, que dicen las cosas llenas
de paja, con mil preámbulos, y rodeos,
pudiéndolo decir en dos palabras, y aun
del *Sinaria copu*, &. Diles á los tales.
*Enopanamansa piculitculit, igcasmong bu-
rimo*.

CULUB. (pp.) *Culuban*. N. S. Cobertera.
V. act. y su prot. Cubrir bueno bueno,
ut cazuela, &. para que no salga el baho.
Abajar. P. 1. pret. *Quilub*, con que ya.
3. Lo que. Mi, T. Mi, P. *Maca*, estar.

CULUBUNG. (pp.) *Mag*, Recíproco, taparse
cara, y todo, *ut* con la manta: y se dice
de las viudas, que andan muy tapadas,
y de los que se velan. *Pagcuculubuñgan:*
pret. *Pigculubuñgan*, 3. la manta, ó luto.
V. act. prot. tapar, cubrir. P. 1. El
con que. 3. pret. *Quilubuñgan*, á quien.
Mi, T. *Maca*, estar. Mi, recíproco.

CULUG. (a.) N. S. Ruido, ó trueno, que
apenas se percibe. V. N. futuro. *Culug*,
Rugir, ó tronar asi, *ut* tripas, ó moris-
queta, cuando hierve, &. *Culugculug*,
frecuentativo.

CULUMBO. (pp.) N. S. Pabellon. *Mag*,
usarle. *Maca*, estar dentro de el. V. act.
poner el pabellon al que ya está dor-
miendo. P. 3. Á quien asi se le pone.
ff. *Paculumbuan, pepaculumbuan*, á quien
se le pone pabellon. *Paculumbuanme iny
Pare*, pon columbo al pare. *Minecucarin
at eraco pepaculumbuan. Paculumbo*, el
que le pone, ó le dá.

CULUMPIS. (pp.) V. N. y su prot. Se-
carse, revenirse, *ut* cañamuda, madera,
que si la ponen verde, luego se reviene,
y se afloja; viejo que se vá secando, &.

CULÚNG. (pp.) V. act. y su prot. Futuro.
Culung, encerrar, *ut* en aposento, corral,
jaula, &. P. 1. pret. *Quilung*, lo que.
Culuñgan, nombre: el lugar, *ut* jaula. *Ma*,
pararse. *Maca*, estar, *ut* monjas, ó pá-
jaros en jaula.

CULUÑYAYAN. (pc.) N. S. Incordios, secos
aunque sea en el pescuezo: prot. salirle.

CULURUN. (pp.) N. S. Arruga, *ut* de frente,
ó ropa. Vide *Culutun:* encojerse.

Figure 17. The Kapampángan word CULIT as it was entered in the 1860 edition of Fray Diego Bergaño's Vocabulario de la Lengua Pampanga en Romance.

consonantal characters possess a default vowel sound that can be altered with the use of diacritical marks (Daniels, 1996). A syllabary on the one hand has a distinct character glyph for each syllable or consonant-vowel compound. A good example of a syllabaries are the Japanese *kana* (*katakana* and *hiragana*) in contrast to Súlat Kapampángan in [Table 1]. In Súlat Kapampángan, the symbol for the consonant sound K (⁓) remains the same in all its vowel combinations, while Japanese

	ka	ki	ku	ke	ko
Japanese (syllabary)	か	き	く	け	こ
Kapampángan (syllabary)	ニ	ニ́	ニ	ニ	ニ

Table 1. Syllabary [Japanese] versus Alphasyllabary [Kapampángan] (Pangilinan 2009 & 2011).

hiragana has a distinct symbol for each consonant-vowel combination. Kulitan is still being mistakenly called *Alibatang Kapampángan* by a number of mis-edcuated Kapampángans who learned the term *alibata* from faulty schoolbooks used in the Philippine educational system. Alibata, believed to be the Filipino term for "alphabet" and used in reference to all native scripts, is actually a 20th century invention and was never an indigenous word. Due to the false notion that the indigenous scripts of the archipelago were derived from Arabic, Paul Versoza, a member of the old National Language Institute, coined the term Alibata in 1914 by combining the first three letters of the Arabic alphabet ١ ALIF, ﺏ BA and ﺕ TA (Versoza, 1939; Morrow, 2002 and Miller, 2011). This term however became part of Philippine education and has yet to be corrected.

The assumption that the Philippine scripts were of Arabic origin has its roots in the beginnings of the Spanish conquest. To the average 16th century Spaniard, strange looking foreign scripts often resembled Arabic writing. This is understandable since the Spaniards experienced the influence of Islamic civilization and religion when they lived under the Moors for 600 years. Since many of the coastal communities they initially encountered in these islands were Muslims, the Spaniards naturally assumed that any form of civilization the natives possessed must have come from the source of their religion, Arabia. Antonio de Morga (1609), a high ranking colonial official, for instance, wrote in his *Sucesos de las Islas Filipinas* that the natives "*escríbese muy bien en todos las islas, con unos caracteres casi como Arábigos,*" and "*á la usanza arábiga.*" Spanish friar Francisco Colín (1663) was more emphatic in his assumptions when he wrote, "it is quite evident that they are all taken from the Moro Malays and originated from the Arabs," (B&R, 1909 and Wade, 1993).

Kulitan or Súlat Kapampángan is also called *Baybayin Kapampángan* by a number of individuals who believed that all Philippine scripts were derived from *Baybayin*, the indigenous Tagalog script. Since the elevation of Tagalog as the basis for the national language in the late 1930s, all the existing languages of the archipelago have been demoted to the status of mere regional dialects (Del Corro, 2000; Gueraiche, 2004; Alunan, 2006; DILA, 2007 and Pangilinan, 2009b). In fact, anything Tagalog has conveniently become equated with anything "national" or "Filipino." A number of individuals are now pushing for Baybayin to legally become the *Pambansang Sulat* or "national script" of the Philippines (National Script Act, 2011; Cabuay, 2011). Once the Tagalog script legally becomes the "national script" of the archipelago, all the existing non-Tagalog indigenous scripts of these islands would suffer the same fate as the indigenous non-Tagalog languages. They will be reduced in importance as mere regional variants of Baybayin and eventually forced to be discarded for the sake of standardization and "national" unity. Like the many existing languages of the archipelago, they would soon become endangered and slowly pushed to extinction.

Although the glyphs used in the Kapampángan and Tagalog scripts share certain similarities in appearance, Súlat Kapampángan has developed unique and distinct character shapes that are different from Baybayin, particularly the consonantal characters Ga (∩), Ta (2), Sa (3) and the plain vertical line for LA (ı) found in several 17th century Kapampángan signatures (Miller, 2010, 2011a & 2012b). Except for the plain vertical line LA (ı), the consistency in shape of the other three characters can be seen in the various *cuadernos* and *abecedarios* that appeared during the Spanish era (Benavente, 1699; Mas, 1842 and Marcilla, 1895), in the *abecedarios* of 20th century Kapampángan writer Zoilo Hilario (1962, and scholar Mariano Henson (1965), as well as in some 17th century Kapampángan documents with Kulitan signatures (Miller, 2010; 2011b and personal communication, December 14, 2011). Súlat Kapampángan also does not interchange the vowels E with I and O with U, as they do in Baybayin (Hilario, 1962; Pangilinan, 1995 & 2009). Also, Kulitan manages to retain the coda consonant as evidenced from the 17th century Kapampángan signatures (Miller 2010 and 2011a), whereas the final consonantal glyph has always been dropped in Tagalog until the introduction of the *virama* or "vowel killer," in the form of a "cross kudlit" by the Spanish friar Francisco López in 1620 (Marcilla, 1895). While most Philippine scripts resemble the Baybayin in form and spelling rules, namely the dropping of the final consonant, Súlat Kapampángan managed to develop its own conventions, as evidenced by several 17th century Kapampángan signatures. In order for Kulitan to develop these spelling conventions differently from Baybayin and other Philippine scripts, it would make sense that Indûng Kapampángan was one of the earliest places where the script was adopted (Miller, 2012).

Kulitan or Súlat Kapampángan could not have been a mere branch of the Tagalog *baybayin* and therefore should never be called *Baybayin Kapampángan*. If anything, Kulitan, or Súlat Kapampángan, could be much older, and may even be the parent script of the Tagalog *baybayin* (Gerona, 2011).

Ó
ZEN
viray
Siuálá ding Meángûbiú
18 ☼ 4 ◑ 2000

PART I

KASALESÁYAN

HISTORY

ÚKULANG PÍBATAN
Origin Theories

Various theories exist regarding the origins of Súlat Kapampángan. Many scholars believed that the various scripts used in these islands, including Kulitan, were ultimately Indian-inspired scripts brought into these islands via Southeast Asian intermediaries. Fletcher Gardner (1869) goes as far as to say that the Philippine scripts might have been invented by travelling Indian priests or scribes who based them on the Brahmi or Karosthi scripts (Wade, 1993). Many scholars do not doubt their Indic origins (Gardner, 1869; Henson, 1965; Francisco, 1973; Scott, 1984 and 1994; Postma, 1990; Wade, 1993; Malaiya, 1997b; Morrow, 2009 and Miller, 2011a & 2011c) [Fig. 18 & 19].

Figure 18. Christopher Ray Miller's Evolution of Philippine Scripts, including Súlat Kapampángan, from Devanagari via Gujarati (Miller, 2011b).

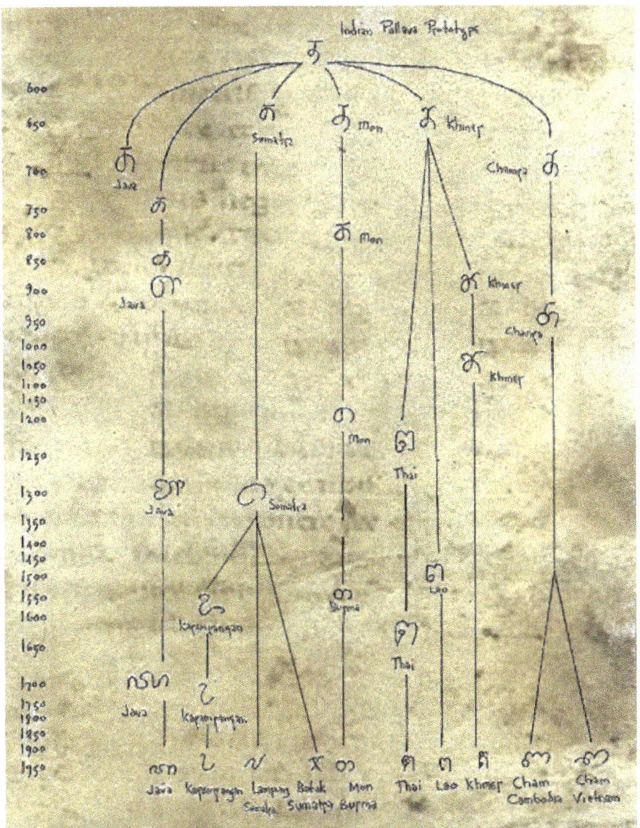

Figure 19. Evolution of Kapampángan and Southeast Asian scripts, modified from the Yashwant Malaiya's 1997 Evolution of Southeast Asian Scripts in Languages and Scripts of India.

Recently though, a number of Philippine nationalistic scholars are beginning to question the external influences regarding the origins of the indigenous scripts. Bonifacio Comandante, Jr. in particular claims that the Baybayin, a term he applies to all Philippine scripts including Kulitan, were an indigenous invention. He postulates that the ancient inhabitants of these islands, who were very much attached to the sea, derived the shapes of the characters in their scripts by observing the natural patterns found on the shells of the taklobo, a species of Tridacna giant clam that are endemic to these islands (Comandante, 2010 & 2011). How he came about this particular assumption is a bit unclear.

To prove that Baybayin was a product of local genius and not of foreign origins, Comandante went further to try and prove that the script was

71

much older than Brahmi, the supposed parent script of all Indic scripts. Scholars postulate that Brahmi was invented around the last centuries before the Common Era. Comandante claims that Baybayin is much older than that.

In his lecture at the *Binalot Talks* hosted by the University of the Philippines Archaeological Studies Program held August 10, 2011, Comandante claimed that the geometric designs on the 3000 year-old Manunggul Jar, currently housed at the National Museum of the Philippines, actually contained hidden Baybayin messages. Those geometric shapes, however, can be anything one wants them to be, in an infinite number of ways.

Comandante further stretched his claims on the antiquity of Baybayin in his presentation at the *Ika-10ng Pambansang BAKAS Seminar-Workshop: "Kasaysayan ng Kapilipinuhan: Bagong Balangkas"*, held at the Don Bosco Technical Institute in Makati on April 19, 2012. He claimed that the five thousand year-old petroglyphs found in a cave in Angono in the province of Rizal depicting various animals, were actually the beginnings of Baybayin. If Comandante is correct, then that would prove Baybayin indeed to be much older than any of the Indic scripts. However, he has yet to connect those drawings to the current shapes of Baybayin characters. Note also that the dating of the Manunggul Jar and the Angono petroglyphs are subject to continuing research.

This speculation that the indigenous scripts of the archipelago were invented locally is not entirely new. In his book *Descriptive Dictionary of the Indian Islands and Adjacent Countries*, John Crawfurd (1856) stated his view that the Philippine Scripts were of local invention. On page 348 of his entry on the *Philippine Archipelago*, Crawfurd wrote, "The form of the character is, moreover, wholly different from that of any Malayan alphabet, and the Philippine writing must, therefore, be deemed indigenous." Geoff Wade (1993) also cited Crawfurd's statement in his *On the Possible Cham Origin of the Philippine Scripts*.

In the early 20th century, Philippine national artist Guillermo Tolentino (1937) wrote a book on the Tagalog language and its indigenous script entitled *Ağ Wika at Baybayiğ Tagalog (Ang Wika at Baybaying Tagalog)*. A Tagalog supremacist, Tolentino believed that Tagalog language and culture was superior and much older than any of the supposed external sources of the Baybayin (Tolentino and Morrow, 2009). He rejects the idea of cultural borrowings from India and the neighboring islands. In his book, Tolentino presents a chart that shows the pictographic and ideographic origins of the Tagalog script (Tolentino, 1937; Morrow, 2009 and Comandante, 2011) [Fig. 20]. Following the same logic, Comandante likewise believed that the Baybayin, and therefore by extension all Philippine scripts, to be much older than their supposed Indic origins. However, Comandante claims his theory to be more cohesive than Tolentino's since he based all forms of scripts on only one source, the Taklobo Giant Clams (Comandante, 2011).

BIGKAS	NGA	WA	PA	YA	DA-RA	NA	GA	SA	KA	MA	TA	LA	HA	BA	O-U	E-I	A
TAGALOG	[glyph]	[glyph]	[glyph]	[glyph]	[glyph]	[glyph]	[glyph]	[glyph]	[glyph]	[glyph]	[glyph]	[glyph]	[glyph]	[glyph]	[glyph]	[glyph]	[glyph]
KAWI (HUWAD SA TAGALOG)	[glyph]	[glyph]	[glyph]	[glyph]	[glyph]	[glyph]	[glyph]	[glyph]	[glyph]	[glyph]	[glyph]	[glyph]	[glyph]	[glyph]	[glyph]	[glyph]	[glyph]
MGA PINAGBUHATANG HUGIS	[glyph]	[glyph]	[glyph]	[glyph]	[glyph]	[glyph]	[glyph]	[glyph]	[glyph]	[glyph]	[glyph]	[glyph]	[glyph]	[glyph]	[glyph]	[glyph]	[glyph]
PANTINIG AT KATINIG NA DULOT NG HUGIS	u NGA	WAKAS	PUNO	AYAN	DAAN	li NALANG	GAWA	SST	KAKABIT	MALAKAS	TIGAS	LALAKE	HANGIN	BABAE	O! HA?	ILOG	oh A
MGA KATUTURAN NG PINAGBUHATAN	ALINGAWNGAW	HANGGAHAN	PUNO'T UGAT	PAGPAPAKITA SA GALAW NG KAMAY	LANGAS	SAINGTINAKPAN	UMA ANG GAWA SA SALITA	PASUWIT, SUTSOT, HINGANG PALABAS	KAKAMBAL, KAUGNAY, KALABAN, KAAWAY	MAKIPANGYARIHAN	TALINO, TALSIK	PAGKA-LALAKE	KIDLAT, BAGYO, HANGIN	PAGNA-BABAE	MAINCHA, TANONG	ILAW, TINIG, TUBIG	PAGIYAK, PAGTUTOL, SIMULA NG BUHAY

Figure 20. Guillermo Tolentino's chart showing the supposed original pictographic and ideographic meanings of the Baybayin taken from his 1937 book Ağ Wika at Baybayiğ Tagalog and reproduced in Bonifacio F. Comandante Jr.'s paper Baybayin Dance: Script Forms Through Time presented at the 1st Philippine Conference on the Ticao Stones on August 5-6, 2011 at Monreal, Masbate, Philippines.

In the same light, a number of Kapampángan nationalists and mystics deny the foreign origins of Kulitan and suggest a purely indigenous source for the script. Many of them believe that the indigenous scripts were taught to them by the *núnû* or ancestral gods, especially the sun god Ápûng Sínukuan. Notice the pictographic origins of the Kulitan, as suggested in [Figures 21 and 22] as well as [Table 2]. One advocate in particular, the Kapampángan musician and composer Ysaganî Yátu Ybarra (Marcelino Sigfried Ranada y Tiglao), insisted that the Kapampángan glyph NGA (ﻉ) was derived from the picture of a *damúlag* (Bubalus bubalis) or water buffalo submerged in a pool of water (Ranada, pers.comm., December 15, 1995). The glyph NGA (ᜅ) clearly shows the etchings of the horns, backbone and tail of the water buffalo. Plus, "nga" sounds like the cry the *damúlag* makes.

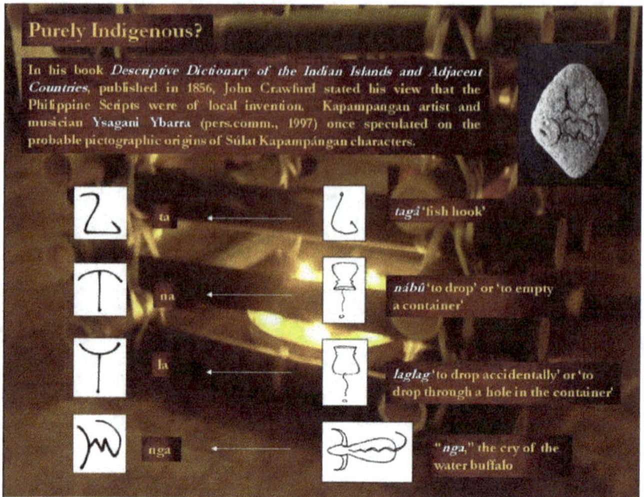

Figure 21. Suggested pictographic origins of Súlat Kapampángan from Slide 11 of Siuálâ ding Meángubié's 2011 lecture on Súlat Kapampángan presented at Holy Angel University in September of 2011.

Figure 22. Suggested pictographic origins of Súlat Kapampángan from Slide 26 of Siuálâ ding Meángubié's 2011 lecture on Súlat Kapampán-gan presented at Holy Angel University in September of 2011.

Character	Sound	Picture	Interpretation
	ta		TA from TAGÂ 'fish hook'
	na		NA from NÁBÛ 'to drop on purpose, to empty a container'
	la		LA from LAGLAG 'to drop off accidentally, to drop off through a hole inside a container"
	nga	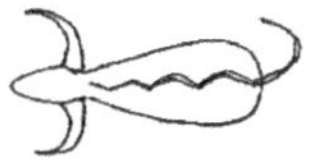	NGA is the sound of the water buffalo. The character represents the top view of a water buffalo (Ranada, M.S.T., pers.comm., December 15, 1995).
	pa		PA from PÂ 'father', the line/stroke outside the vessel/dipper represents the male reproductive organ.
	ma		MA from MÂ 'mother', the line/stroke inside the vessel/dipper represents the female reproductive organ.
	ba		BA from BÍLUG 'circle'

Table 2. Pictographic origins of Súlat Kapampángan (Pangilinan, 2002, 2008, 2009 & 2011).

The idea that the indigenous scripts of these islands were of local invention was however put into question when compared to the Indian-inspired Kawi script (old Javanese) used in the 10th century Laguna Copper Plate Inscription (LCI) that is currently housed at the National Museum [Fig. 23]. The LCI was discovered accidentally during the dredging of the Lumbang River in Laguna in 1987. It was proven to be authentic by both local and international scholars. The LCI itself bears the Saka date 822 that is equivalent to 900 C.E. (Postma, 1990). It is therefore the oldest textual evidence of Indic influence in the archipelago to date (Wade, 1993). It contains a number of Sanskrit names and titles, particularly the 10th century ruler of Tondo, who styled himself with the Dharma name Jayadeva [ꦧꦗꦢꦺꦮ] and the Sanskrit title for admiral, Senapati [ꦱꦺꦤꦥꦠꦶ] (Postma, 1990). It also contains place names that were once a traditional part of the Kapampángan homeland.

Figure 23. The 10th century C.E. Laguna Copper Plate Inscription (LCI) written in Kawi (ancient Javanese) is by far considered the oldest written document in the Philippines. It is currently housed at the National Museum of the Philippines. 2009 photo of the LCI in situ at the National Museum courtesy of Roslyn Arayata's Site: http://zestybliss.wordpress.com/category/published-work-photograph/.

Tondo, for instance, was once said to speak the same language as the Kapampángan nation (Loarca, 1583; B&R, 1905 and Tayag, 1985). Most likely it shared the same writing system as well. Many of the character shapes in Kulitan, including those believed to be of local invention, are very similar to the Indian-inspired Kawi script used in the LCI [Table 3].

Sound	Brahmi (Parent Script of all Indic Scripts)	Devanagari	Kawi (Javanese)	Burmese	Hangul (Korean)	Kulitan (Kapampangan)	Tagbanua	Baybayin (Tagalog)
GA	∧	ग	∏	∩	ㄱ	⌒	⟨glyph⟩	⟨glyph⟩
KA	+	क	⫫	∽	ㅋ	=	×	⟨glyph⟩
TA (DA)[1]	⊂	ट	⟨glyph⟩	∞	ㄷ	⟨glyph⟩	⟨glyph⟩	⟨glyph⟩
DA (JA)[2]	⟨glyph⟩	द	E	ϡ	E	⟨glyph⟩	⟨glyph⟩	⟨glyph⟩
MA (BA)[3]	⟨glyph⟩	म	⟨glyph⟩	⟨glyph⟩	ㅂ	⟨glyph⟩	⟨glyph⟩	⟨glyph⟩
PA	⟨glyph⟩	प	∪	∪	ㅍ	⟨glyph⟩	⟨glyph⟩	⟨glyph⟩
BA (MA)*	□	ब	⟨glyph⟩	⟨glyph⟩	ㅁ	○	○	⟨glyph⟩

Table 3. Kulitan or Súlat Kapampángan in comparison with other Indic scripts.

NB: 1 Read as DA in Kawi (Javanese) and Hangul (Korean). 2 Read as JA in Brahmi (Indian) and Kawi (Javanese). 3 Read as BA in Hangul (Korean). *Read as MA in Hangul (Korean).

Moreover, Kulitan, like the Kawi used in the LCI, is an *abugida* (Pangilinan, 2009) It shows striking similarities with the rules of Brahmi [Table 4], which is said to be the parent script of all Indian-inspired abugida throughout Southeast Asia (Gardner, 1943; Wade, 1993 and Malaiya, 1997a). Like Brahmi, the consonantal glyphs in Kulitan possess the inherent vowel sound "A". This default vowel sound can also be altered with the use of vocalic indicators placed above or below the consonantal characters.

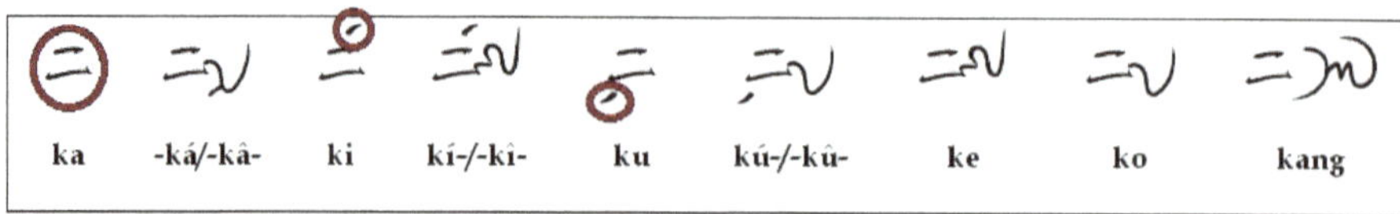

| ka | -ká/-kâ- | ki | kí-/-kì- | ku | kú-/-kû- | ke | ko | kang |

Súlat Kapampángan

| ka | kā | ki | kī | ku | kū | ke | ko | kaṃ |

Brahmi Script

Table 4. Similarities between Súlat Kapampángan and Brahmi (Pangilinan, 2002, 2008 & 2009). The Kapampangan true type fonts used are by Norman de los Santos (2011).

If there is ample evidence to prove that Kulitan is an Indian-inspired script, the problem is how it was brought to Indûng Kapampángan. Was Kulitan invented by Indian priests or scribes who travelled to these shores as suggested by Gardner (1869)? Is it purely a local invention as Crafurd (1856) suggested? Or could it have been invented locally on the basis of other Indian-inspired scripts brought to these shores from the neighboring islands? This would explain the presence of glyphs similar to other Indian-inspired scripts in combination with glyphs the shapes of which are unique to Súlat Kapampángan. Or could it be that Kulitan was invented by local scholars who travelled abroad and were influenced by Indian-inspired culture, particularly by Tantric Buddhism at the capital of Srivijaya in Sumatra at about the same period as the LCI (Pangilinan, 2008 and 2009)? Srivijaya was a Buddhist empire located in the island of Java and South Sumatra in the 7th to the 13th century C.E. (Yijing [義淨], 695; Coedes, 1918; Satyawati, 1980 and 1981).

In 670 AD, the Buddhist Empire of Srivijaya assumed complete control of the Straits of Malacca, the main maritime trade route between India and China (Coedes, 1918). It was in control for about 640 years. Its capital in Suwarnadvipa (Sumatra) became the center of trade and learning in Tantric Buddhism (Vajrayana). Scholars from as far as China and India came to Sumatra to study under the Buddhist masters like the Sumatran prince Dharmarakshita, who was venerated as great Buddhist saint Serlingpa in Tibetan Buddhism (Yijing [義淨], 695; Satyawati,

1980 and 1981). Tibet owes the revival of its Buddhism to Atisha and his Sumatran master Serlingpa (Dharmarakshita) who reintroduced Tantric Buddhism to Tibet after its persecution in the 10th century C.E. (Berzin, 2003). Now Tantric Buddhism exists in Tibet and Japan, thanks to the empire of Srivijaya in Sumatra. If Srivjaya's influence spread as far as China, India and Tibet, then why not to the Kingdom of Luzon and the other ancient states within the archipelago?

During roughly the same era, travelling Buddhist monks were inventing scripts for a number of nations that did not have a written language. For instance, the Tibetan Buddhist monk Phagspa invented a script for Kublai Khan in 1269 C.E., which became the official script of the Mongol Empire (West, 2006b). It was an abugida based on the Indian-inspired Tibetan script. Two hundred years later, the Buddhist monk Syol Chong invented the Korean script Hangul for King Sejong in 1446 C.E. (Malaiya, 1997c and Ledyard, 1998). Also an abugida, Hangul was based on a number of Indian-inspired scripts, namely the Mongol script invented by Phagspa and Tibetan. It was at first used to facilitate the reading of Buddhist scriptures. Later it was modified to become Korea's official script. In the same light, Kulitan may have been invented by Kapampángan scholars who travelled and studied at the Buddhist capital of Srvijaya in Sumatra at around the same period. Notice the similarity between Kulitan and other Indian-inspired Asian scripts [Table 3] and the structure and format of scripts invented by Buddhist monks [Fig. 24]. This may explain why Philippine paleographer Juan R. Francisco (1973) wrote in his *Philippine Paleography* that "there is a high degree of correspondence between Sumatran and Philippine Indic scripts" and that the indigenous scripts of these islands "belong to the same family as the Sumatran systems" (Wade, 1993). If Srivijaya's influence was felt in Southeast Asia to as far as China, India and Tibet, it is quite unlikely that its influence never reached the archipelago. The unearthing of Tantric Buddhist artifacts like the Golden Tara in Agusan, the Padmapani medallion in Batangas, the Golden Garuda from Brooke's Point in Palawan and the Lokesvara image of Cebu might help corroborate the existence of Srivijayan contact into these islands (Francisco, 1971 and 1981). Also, the oldest artifact ever found in Indûng Kapampángan is the 5000 year old Candaba stone adze used for building boats, implying that the early inhabitants were navigators (Dizon, Eusebio, pers.comm., October 2000). If the early Kapampángans who were one of the Luçoes or "people of Luzon" were recorded by the Portuguese as explorers and adventurers, then it is highly unlikely that their ancestors never set foot in Srvijaya.

Figure 24, Súlat Kapampángan in comparison to other Indian-inspired Asian scripts developed by Buddhist monks from the 6th to 15th century C.E. Taken from Slide 13 of Siuálâ ding Meángubié's 2011 lecture on Súlat Kapampángan presented at Holy Angel University in September of 2011.

The intercourse between Sumatra and Indûng Kapampángan was noted during the early years of the Spanish conquest. In his *Labor Evangelica*, Fray Francisco Colin (1663) wrote that he met a Kapampángan in the Moluccas who claimed to have encountered an old Kapampángan village by a huge lake deep in the heart of the island of Sumatra (B&R, 1905 and Henson, 1965). Kapampángan advocate Abraham Tayag was convinced that this lake was Danau Toba which is situated at the heartland of the Batak nation in Sumatra (Tayag, pers.comm., August 24, 2001). Incidentally, the Batak nation shares striking similarities with the myths and folklores of the Kapampángan nation. Like the Kapampángan, the Batak believe that originally there were two suns that constantly fought each other (Loeb, 1935; Fansler, 1921 and Pangilinan, 2000). They also believe that the eclipse is caused by the *Láwû*, that is Sanskrit *ráhû*

80

(राहुः), a mythical demon that swallows the sun or the moon (Loeb, 1935; Bergaño, 1732; Panganiban, 1972 and Joosten, 2001). Striking similarities between the languages and cultures of the various Sumatran nations and the Kapampángan nation can also be read from William Marsden's *The History of Sumatra* published in 1811.

William Henry Scott (1994) wrote that the *Luçoes* or "people of Luzon" were once actively involved in the wars and politics in the Straits of Malacca in the 16th century C.E., particularly in the wars involving the Sumatran states of Atjeh, Batak and Menangkabau. The Kapampángan nation who were one of the *Luçoes*, then already had a close and regular intercourse with the various states in the island of Sumatra long before the coming of the Europeans. This may explain not just the similarities in language and culture between Kapampángan and the various Sumatran nations but also the high degree of correspondence between Sumatran and the indigenous scripts of the archipelago, including Kulitan, as noted by Francisco (1973).

BAKAS NING MILÁBAS
Historical Specimens

Perhaps the oldest evidence of Kulitan were the markings found in the *ruson tsubo* (呂宋壺) or Luzon jars exported to Japan by the Kingdom of Luzon in the 16th century that Tauchi Yonesaburo (田内米三郎) mentioned in his book *Tokiko* (陶器考) [Fig. 14]. He called them *ruson koku ji* (呂宋國字) or the "writing of the Kingdom of Luzon" (Tauchi [田内], 1853 and Cole, 1912). Tauchi did not include any actual photographs, most likely it was impossible in 1853 Japanese publications. Unfortunately, I did not have enough clout and authority to inspect the bottom of the Luzon jars in the various museums I visited in Japan. It was unthinkable for the curators, every time I asked to see the bottom.

One of the oldest handwriting specimens written by a Kapampángan during the early part of the Spanish conquest in the late 16th century is the signature of Don Dionisio Capulong, son of the *Lakandúlâ* of Tondo and ruler of Candaba.

Several specimens can be found in the archives of the University of Santo Tomas in Manila. They were perhaps written between 1594 up to the time of his death in 1607, the years he collaborated with the Spaniards upon his return from exile in Mexico (Santiago, 1990a). The following specimens [Fig. 25 & 26] were the presentation by Christopher Ray Miller (2011b) at the University of Santo Tomas, entitled *Filipino Cultural Heritage in the UST Archives: Baybayin scripts in 17th century land deeds*.

Figure 14. Map of Pampanga from Pedro Murillo Velarde's 1744 Mapa de las Islas Filipinas. The Pampanga Delta Region had been inaccurately assigned to Bulacan.

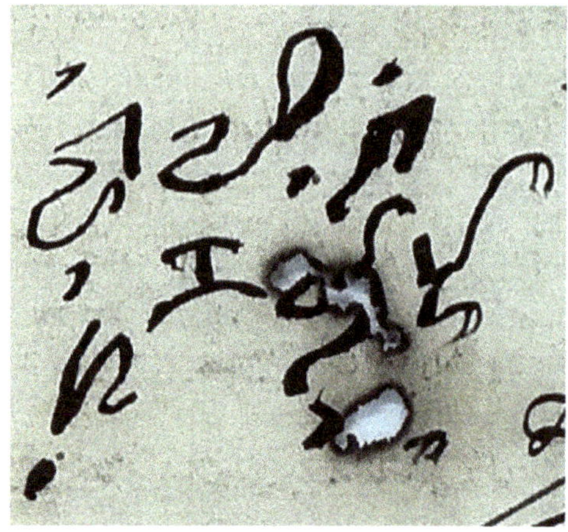

Figure 25. Signature of Don Dionisio Capulong, son of Lakandúlâ, ruler of Candaba. In Filipino Cultural Heritage in the UST Archives: Baybayin scripts in 17th century land deeds (Miller, 2011b).

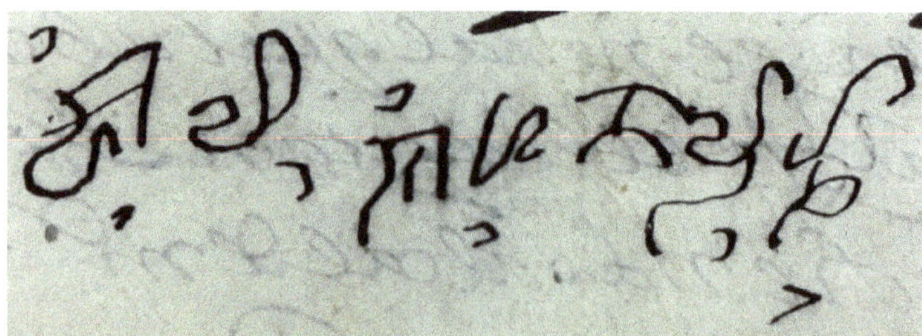

Figure 26. Signature of Don Dionisio Capulong, son of Lakandúlâ, ruler of Candaba. In Filipino Cultural Heritage in the UST Archives: Baybayin scripts in 17th century land deeds (Miller, 2011b).

Another set of old Kapampángan handwriting specimens come from two 17th century documents originally given by Antoon Postma to Jean-Paul Potet and passed on to me courtesy of Christopher Ray Miller (2010). One document was dated August 16, 1617 C.E. [Fig. 27] and the other September 13, 1632 [Fig. 28].

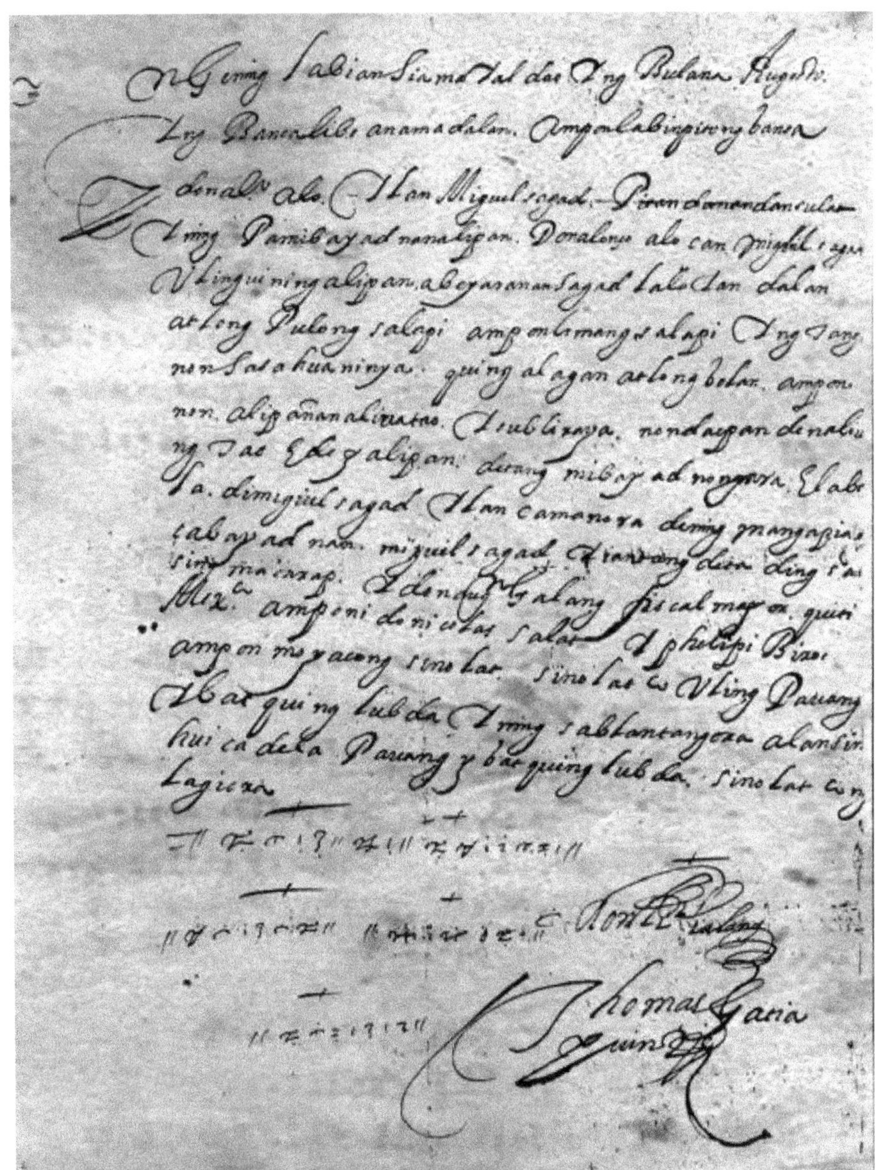

Figure 27. A notarized Kapampángan document which served as a deed to the sale of a slave dated September 16, 1617. The names of five individuals was signed in Kulitan. Photo courtesy of Christopher Ray Miller (pers.comm., July 10, 2011).

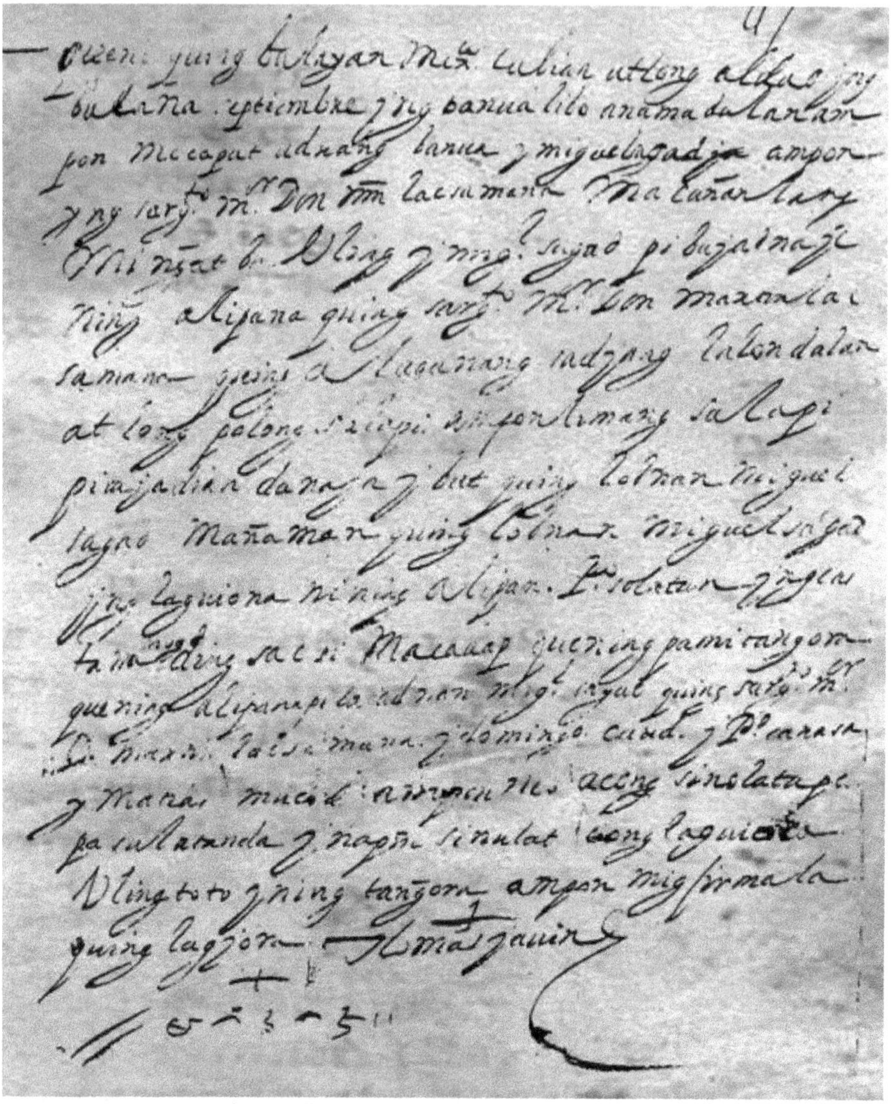

Figure 28. A Kapampángan document that served as a deed to the sale of a slave dated September 13, 1632 in Mexico, Pampanga and signed in Kulitan at the bottom left corner by Miguel Sagad. Photo courtesy of Christopher Ray Miller (pers. comm., July 10, 2011).

The notarized documents are deeds to the sale of a slave. What is interesting in these documents is the retention of the final consonantal glyph which is always absent in Tagalog Baybayin until the introduction of the *virama* or vowel killer in the form of a "cross *kudlit*" by Spanish friar Francisco López in 1620 (Miller, 2010 & 2011a). Other interesting details are the unusual shapes of some of the glyphs that are quite different from the usual similar shapes found in the *abecedarios* of Benavente (1699), Mas (1843) and Marche (1887) found in Marcilla (1895) (Miller, 2010 and 2011a). The glyph LA (т) appear only as a plain vertical line ('). Don Alonso Alo's vowel glyph A (⚹) has an interesting shape compared to the usual A (⌵) [Fig. 29]. Miguel Sagad's final consonant syllable DA (⚶) is also interesting compared to the usual DA (⚵) [Fig. 30]. A closer view of the 1617 signature of Phelipe Biruc is also added for cross reference [Fig. 31].

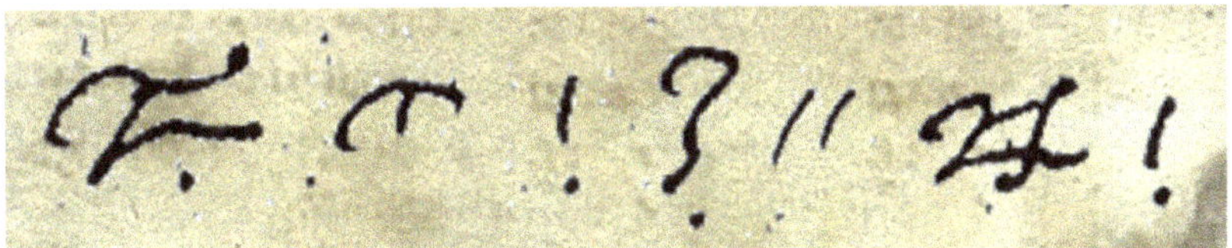

Figure 29. Here is a closer look at Don Alonso Alô's signature taken from the 1617 Kapampángan document courtesy of Christopher Ray Miller (pers. comm. July 10, 2011). Notice how the initial A of his name Alonso coalesced with the final N of Don (Miller, 2010). Notice also the unique shape of his A in Alô and plain vertical lines that stands for the L in the LU of Alunsu (Alonso) and Alu (Alo).

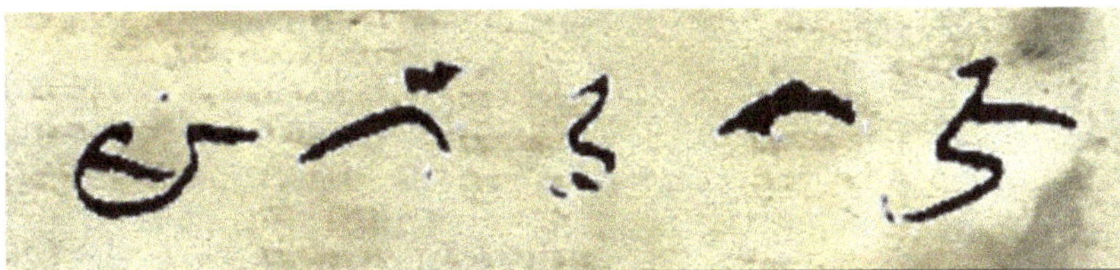

Figure 30. Here is a closer look at Miguel Sagad's signature taken from the 1632 Kapampángan document courtesy of Christopher Ray Miller (pers. comm. July 10, 2011). Notice the presence of the final consonant D in his name which is commonly dropped in Baybayin and other Philippine scripts till the introduction of the "cross kudlit" that acted as virama (vowel killer) by Fray Francisco López in 1620.

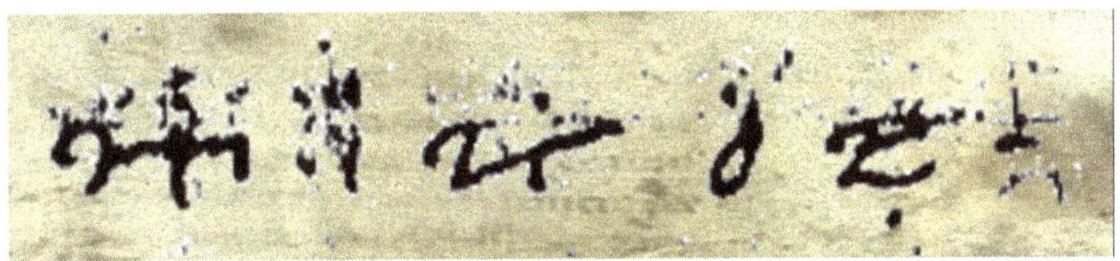

Figure 31. Here is a closer look at Phelipe Biruc's signature taken from the 1617 Kapampángan document courtesy of Christopher Ray Miller (pers. comm. July 10, 2011). The slightly faded final consonant K is nevertheless retained in his surname Biruk (Biruc) where it would have been dropped in Baybayin or retained with Fray Lopez's "cross kudlit".

The next set of historical handwritten Kulitan specimens come from the Manila Archdiocesan Archives. They are the handwritten signatures from the Kapampángan nobility who came to Manila in 1621 to act as witnesses for the beatification of Madre Doña Jeronima de la Asuncion who founded the Monastery of Santa Clara (Santiago, 2002).

These Kapampángan nobles who signed their names in the indigenous script were recorded as Doña Luisa Yosto of Macabebe, Doña Isabel Pangisnauan of Mexico (Masíku) and Don Pablo Maniud, also of Mexico (Masíku). The following images, [Fig. 32, 33 & 34], have been faithfully reproduced by Christopher Ray Miller (2011d) from the original documents and posted on the wall of the Facebook group KULITAN (Indigenous Kapampángan Script).

The oldest existing abecedary and primer on how to read and write Kulitan appear in Fray Alvaro de Benavente's *Vocabulario de Lengua Pampanga* that was published in 1699 [Fig. 35]. So far, Benavente was the first to use the name *culit* in reference to the characters used in Kapampángan writing. The first half of the first chapter of his book was devoted to introducing and explaining how to read and write each of the characters. One curious note is his mention of the use of the Tagalog character ↶ to represent the H sound which does not exist in the Kapampángan language except in loan words. However, Benavente did not include it in his abecedary. Another interesting note in his primer that makes Súlat Kapampángan different from Tagalog *Baybayin* is the way Kapampángans used the vowels "I" and "U" in place of the consonantal characters Y and W respectively. The Kapampángans seemed to have discarded the use of the latter characters, although Kapampángan vowel glyph U (∨) very much resembles the Tagalog consonantal glyph Wa (∂) (Miller, 2011b). Kapampángan vowel glyph I (ℕ) can also be altered to form the sound "Yi" by placing a diacritical mark above it, (ℕ), while the "Yu" sound is formed by placing the diacritical mark under it, (ℕ). In the same manner, the consonantal glyph U (∨) can be also be altered by placing a diacritical mark above or below it. The sound "Wi" is represented by the vowel glyph U with a diacritical mark on top, (∨̇), while the sound "Wu" can be represented by placing a diacritical mark below the vowel glyph U (∨̣).

Figure 32. The 1621 signature of a Kapampángan noble woman, Doña Luisa Yosto of Meacabebe, faithfully copied from the original document at the Manila Archdiocesan Archives by Christopher Ray Miller (2011d).

Figure 33. The 1621 signature of a Kapampángan noble woman, Doña Isabel Pangisnauan of Mexico, Indûng Kapampángan, faithfully copied from the original document at the Manila Archdiocesan Archives by Christopher Ray Miller (2011d). Notice the final consonant N in the surname Pangisnauan, a feature unique to Kapampángan writing.

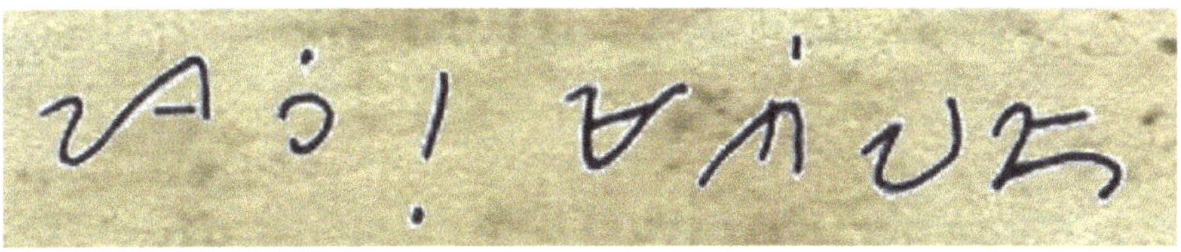

Figure 34. The 1621 signature of a Kapampángan noble, Don Pablo Maniud of Mexico, Indûng Kapampángan, faithfully copied from the original document at the Manila Archdiocesan Archives by Christopher Ray Miller (2011d). Notice the final consonant D in the surname Maniud, a feature unique to Kapampángan writing.

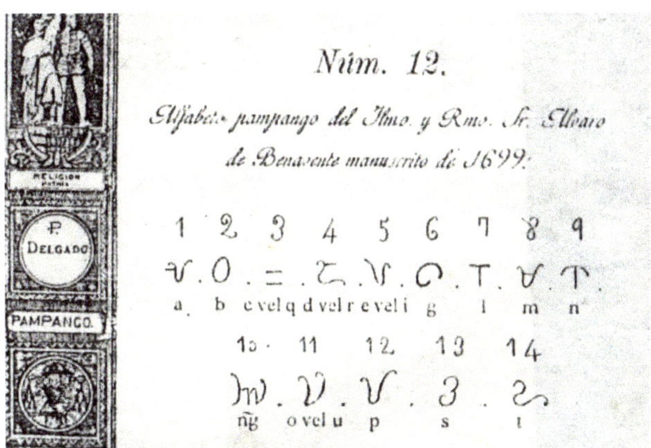

Figure 35. The CULIT described by Fray Diego de Benavente in his 1699 Arte de la Lengua Pampanga, reproduced here in Fray Cipriano Marcilla's 1895 Estudio de los Antiguos Alfabetos Filipinos.

Other abecedaries would appear in the course of the Spanish era. These includes the abecedary of Sinibaldo de Mas (1843) and Alfred Marche (1887) which were reproduced in Cipriano Marcilla's *Estudio de los Antiguos Alfabetos Filipinos* published in 1895 [Fig. 36 & 37].

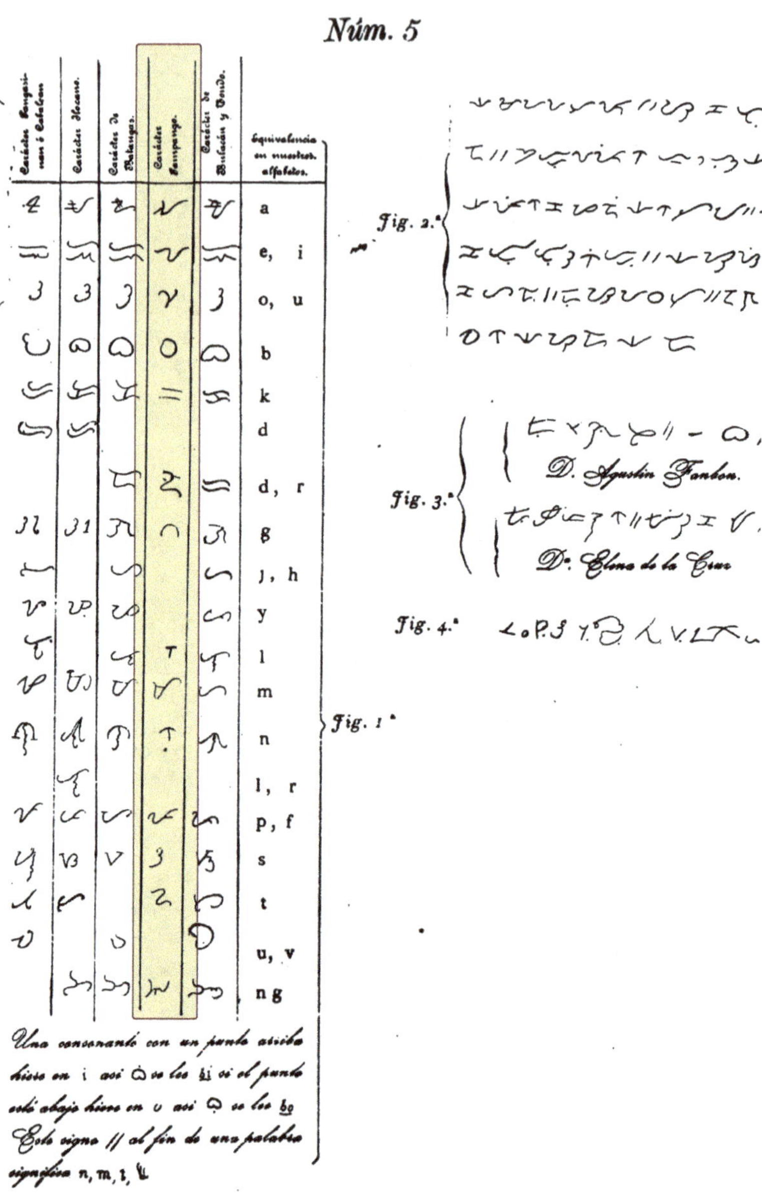

Figure 36. The "Carácter Pampango" by Sinibaldo de Mas in his Informe sobre el estado de las Islas Filipinas en 1842, reproduced here in Fray Cipriano Marcilla's 1895 Estudio de los Antiguos Alfabetos Filipinos.

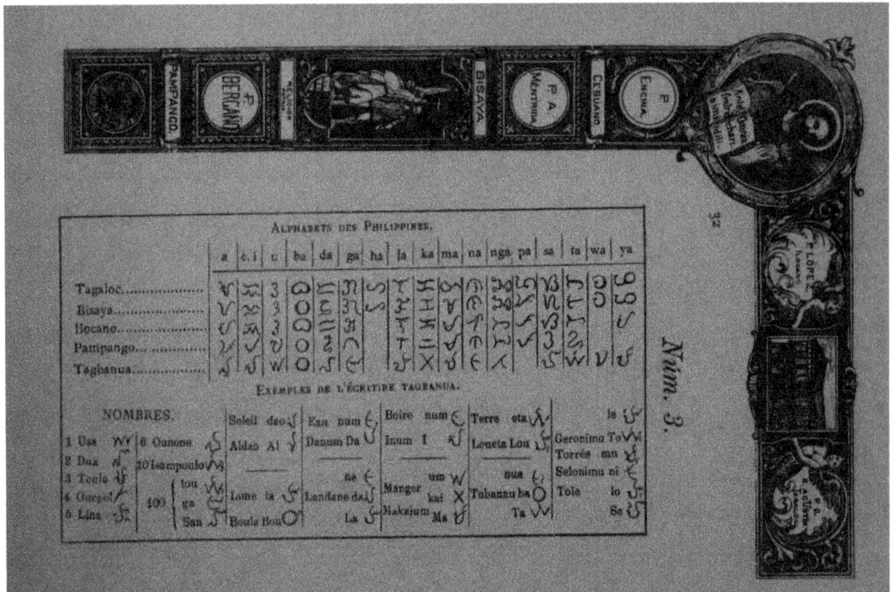

Figure 37. A comparison of Philippine scripts recorded by Alfred Marche (1887) reproduced here in Fray Cipriano Marcilla's 1895 Estudio de los Antiguos Alfabetos Filipinos..

In the 20th century, Kapampángan nationalist writer Zoilo Hilario (1962) of the Akademyang Kapampángan also prepared an abecedary [Fig. 38] and a primer in his typed-written work *Báyung Súnis*. Hilario devoted his chapter on orthography entitled *Tuntunan king Pamisulatmap* on the indigenous Kapampángan script vis-à-vis his proposed indigenized orthography when writing Kapampángan in the Latin script. In explaining how to read and write Kulitan, Hilario was able to present its uniqueness compared to other scripts, particularly to Tagalog, in several sections of this chapter. For instance, in section 14, Hilario wrote, *"Makayaliwà king Tagálug, ing Kapampángan atin yang aduang kulit a máging metung mû"* [The difference with Tagalog is that Kapampángan possess two kulit (glyphs) that become one]. He was referring to the distinct vowel sounds E and O in Kapampángan that are actually the monopthongized diphthongs of AI and AU respectively. Other Philippine scripts do not have a distinct symbols for these sounds that is why they simply interchange E with I and O with U. In Kapampángan, these sounds are clear and distinct and must still be written as diphthongs. He wrote further on section 15, *"Alang kulit a kakatnì karing salitang pilipinu a agauà mung metung mû"* [There are no kulit (glyphs) to represent the monophtongized diphthongs in other Philippine languages (scripts).]. With regards to the vowel glyphs I (ᴎ) and U (ᴠ), Hilario repeats Benavente (1699) on how they can also stand for the consonant sounds Y and W respectively. This is also the reason why Hilario finds no problem in using the Y and W in his proposed indigenized orthography when writing the Kapampángan language in the Latin script. In the old Spanish-style orthography preferred by Kapampángan writers from Bacúlud (Bacolor), the letter W is absent while the letter Y is only used in the initial position or when it stands alone. In the last section of this chapter, Hilario wrote that the Kapampángan word for *kudlit*, the diacritical marks used in altering the default vowel sounds in the shape of dots or apostrophe, is *garlit*.

Renowned Kapampángan scholar and historian Mariano A. Henson (1965) however adds the consonant glyphs YA (ↄ₂) and WA (ᵔ) to his abecedary as distinct from his vowel glyphs I (ᵛ) and U (ᴗ) [Fig. 39] His abecedary is included in the final 1965 edition of his book *Pampanga and Its Towns*. Henson was also the first to present a list of the Kapampángan consonant characters with their default vowel sound A.

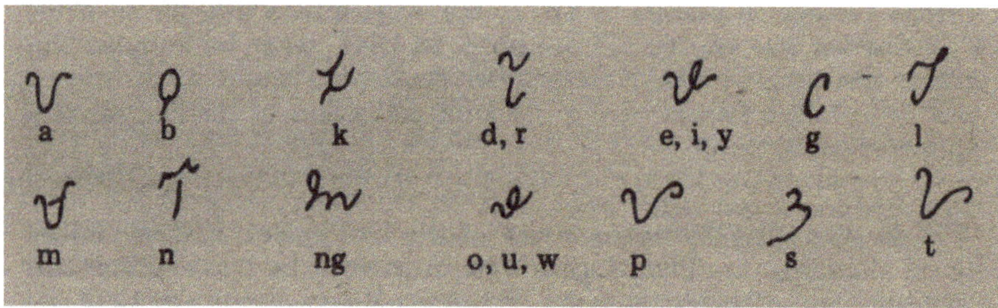

Figure 38. Zoilo Hilario's abecedary from his 1962 typscript Báyung Súnis.

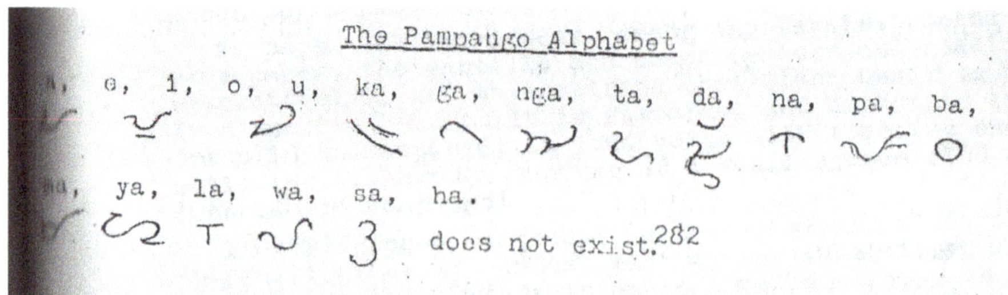

Figure 39. Mariano Henson's abecedary from his 1965 book The Province of Pampanga and Its Towns: A.D. 1300-1965..

PART II

PÁMAGKULIT

WRITING RULES

INDÛ AT ANAK
Mother and Child

Kulitan is basically made up of INDUNG SÚLAT or the "mother" characters and the ANAK SÚLAT or the "offspring" characters. The *Indûng Súlat* are the base characters with the unaltered inherent vowel sounds. They are the building blocks of *Súlat Kapampángan*. *Indûng Súlat* gives birth to *Anak Súlat* or "offspring" characters whenever their inherent vowel sound has been altered by a ligature or a diacritical mark.

The SIWÁLÂ or vowels in *Súlat Kapampángan* are usually written as *garlit* or diacritical marks placed above or below an individual *Indûng Súlat*. Ligatures are also sometimes used to further lengthen these vowel sounds. A glyph with a diacritical mark or ligature attached to it is an *Anak Súlat*.

The *Indûng Súlat* characters are divided into two groups: the consonantal glyphs or KULIT A SISIWÁLÂ (KULIT A MÁGKAS in the first edition) or KULIT A MAKIKATNÎ (Hilario, 1962) and the independent vowel glyphs or KULIT A SIWÁLÂ. The *Kulit a Siwálâ* can stand are usually written in the initial position. They are not the same as the *garlit*.

The recital order of the INDÛNG SÚLAT or basic mother characters are A, I, U, E, O, GA, KA, NGA, TA, DA, NA, LA, SA, MA, PA, BA.

INDUNG SÚLAT: DING KULIT A SISIWÁLÂ
The Consonantal Characters

There are eleven *Kulit a Sisiwálâ* or consonantal glyphs in Kulitan, the recital order of which are GA, KA, NGA, TA, DA, NA, LA, SA, MA, PA, BA. They are however arranged and usually grouped together as follows [Table 5]:

ibat lábî	ihat lábî ibat lábî	ibat akmúlan
ma pa	da/ra ta na la	ga ka
sasaldak	sasalitsit	dalan árung
ba	sa	nga

Table 5. The *Kulit a Sisiwálâ* or Kulitan consonantal characters in their natural arrangement, read from the right column going to the left.

a. *Kulit ngágkas king akmúlan* (velar): GA (∩) and KA (≍).

b. *Kulit ngágkas king árung* (nasal): NGA (ᴐᴵ).

c. *Kulit ngágkas king ípan* (dental): TA (Ɀ) and NA (Ƭ).

d. *Kulit ngágkas king ípan a déla king dílâ* (alveolar):
DA/RA (Ʒ) and LA (Ƭ).

e. *Kulit ngágkas pasalitsit king ípan* (fricative): SA (Ɜ).

f. *Kulit ngágkas king lábî* (bilabial): MA (Ӌ) and PA (Ӌ).

g. *Kulit ngágkas patiúp king lábî* (aspirated bilabial): BA(O).

WA and YA are considered *Télasiwálâ* 'semi-vowels' in Kapampángan and are created from vowel glyphs U (ʋ) and I (ل) respectively (Benavente, 1699 and Hilario, 1962). Like their consonant counterparts, the vowel glyphs U (ʋ) and I (ل) can be altered by placing a *garlit* or diacritical mark above or below the glyph to form "offspring" characters or *Anak Súlat*. This will be explained further in the following sections of this chapter.

While all other glyphs in the other indigenous scripts within the archipelago resemble one another, Kulitan has also developed unique and distinct character shapes that are different from Baybayin, particularly the *Kulit Sisiwálâ* or consonantal characters GA (∩), TA (Ɀ), SA (Ɜ) that are consistent in appearance in the various *cuadernos* and *abecedarios* that have appeared during the Spanish era (Benavente, 1699; Mas, 1842 and Marcilla, 1895) and the modern era (Hilario, 1962, Henson, 1965 and Pangilinan, 1995), and the plain vertical line for LA (ɩ) found in several 17th century Kapampángan signatures (Miller, 2010

INDÛNG SÚLAT: KULIT A SIWÁLÂ
The Vowel Characters

For vowels as *Indûng Súlat* or independent syllable glyphs, Kulitan has three basic *Kulit a Siuálâ* or vowel characters. These are A (𑚁), I (𑚂) and U (𑚃).

However, the Kapampángan language has two monophthongized diphthongs (Gonzales, 1972). These became the vowels E and O and are represented by the "*aduang kulit a máging metung mû*" (Hilario, 1962) or *Miyasáuang Kulit* or "married" or "coupled" vowels E (𑚅) and O (𑚆) [Table 6]. Unlike other Philippine languages, the Kapampángan language does not interchange the vowels I and E since E is a monophthongized diphthong. Kapampángan words ending in the vowel E like *bale* (house), *pále* (unhusked rice) and *sále* (nest) used to be pronounced as *balai*, *pálai* and *sálai*. Thus the vowel E is still written as AI (𑚅) in Kulitan. Likewise, the Kapampángan language does not interchange the vowels U with O since O is also a monophthongized diphthong. The Kapampángan words that end in O like *bábo* (above), *sabó* (soup or juice) and *ulimó* (tiger) all used to be pronounced as *bábau*, *sabáu* and *ulimau*. Thus the vowel O is still written as AU (𑚆) in Kulitan.

The *Kambal Siuálâ* or "twin" vowels seen on Table 6 represent the lengthening of the vowel sounds and the glottal stops in the Kapampángan language. These are usually represented by the diacritical marks *sakúrut* (´) and *télaturung* (^) when writing the Kapampángan language in the Latin script. When they stand alone, the *kambal siuálâ* or "twin" vowels are as follows: –Á-/-Â (𑚋), -Í-/-Î (𑚌) and –Ú-/-Û (𑚍).

kambal siwálâ	miyasáwang siwálâ	siwálâ

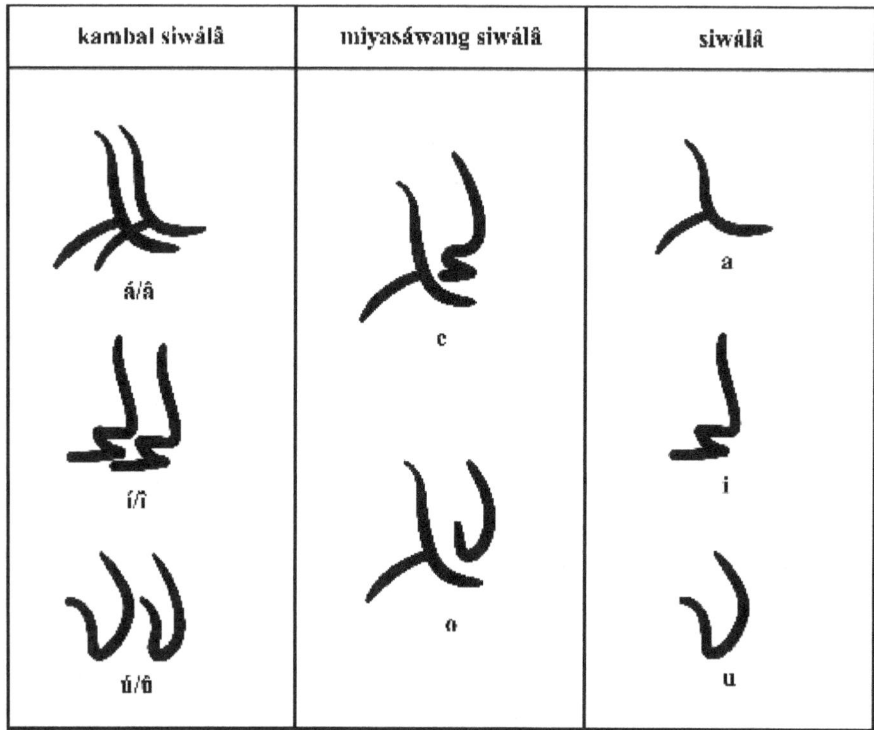

Table 6. The kulit a siuálâ or Kulitan vowel glyphs.

ANAK SÚLAT
The Offspring Characters

As mentioned earlier, all of the consonantal characters in Kulitan possess the inherent vowel sound 'A'. On their own they are known as *Indûng Súlat* or mother characters. To alter their default vowel sounds and produce *Anak Súlat* or offspring characters, one simply places the *garlit* or diacritical marks above or below or place a ligature character next to the mother character. Again, the *Anak Súlat* or offspring characters are those characters with their inherent vowel sounds altered by the diacritical marks or ligatures [Table 7a & 7b].

Indung Súlat	Anak Súlat							
sa	sá/sâ	si	sí/sî	su	sú/sû	se	so	sang
৩	৩৲	৩	৩৶	৩	৩৲	৩৶	৩৴	৩৴

Table 7a. The anak súlat or offspring characters of the indûng súlat SA (৩).

Indûng Súlat	Anak Súlat								
Default	a	-á-/-â	i	-í-/-î	u	-ú-/-û	e	o	-ng
a							e	o	ang
i	ya	-yá-/-yâ	yi	-yí-/-yî	yu	-yú-/-yû	ye	yo	yang
u	wa	-wá-/-wâ	wi	-wí-/-wî	wu	-wú-/-wû	we	wo	wang
e									eng
o									ong
ga		-gá-/-gâ	gi	gi-/-gî	gu	-gú-/-gû	ge	go	gang
ka		-ká-/-kâ	ki	-kí-/-kî	ku	-kú-/-kû	ke	ko	kang
nga		-ngá-/-ngâ	ngi	-ngi-/-ngî	ngu	-ngú-/-ngû	nge	ngo	ngang
ta		-tá-/-tâ	ti	-tí-/-tî	tu	-tú-/-tû	te	to	tang
da		-dá-/-dâ	di	-dí-/-dî	du	-dú-/-dû	de	do	damg
na		-ná-/-nâ	ni	-ní-/-nî	nu	-nú-/-nû	ne	no	nang
la		-lá-/-lâ	li	-lí-/-lî	lu	-lú-/-lû	le	lo	lang
sa		-sá-/-sâ	si	-sí-/-sî	su	-sú-/-sû	se	so	sang
ma		-má-/-mâ	mi	-mí-/-mî	mu	-mú-/-mû	me	mo	mang
pa		-pá-/-pâ	pi	-pí-/-pî	pu	-pú-/-pû	pe	po	pang
ba		-bá-/-bâ	bi	-bí-/-bî	bu	-bú-/-bû	be	bo	bang

Table 7b. Table of Indûng Súlat and their Anak Súlat

PÁMANGANAK NING INDÛNG
SÚLAT KING SIUÁLÂNG [I]
Changing the default vowel sound 'A' to 'I'

To change the default 'A' sound of any of the consonantal characters
to 'I', simply place a *garlit* or diacritical mark above it. For example,
Indûng Súlat KA (ニ) becomes *Anak Súlat* KI (ニ) by placing the *garlit*
(') above it.

Example diagram:

ya	yi	yu	ye	yo	yá/yâ	yí/wî	yú/yû

PÁMANGANAK NING INDÛNG
SÚLAT KING SIWÁLÂNG [U]
Changing the default vowel sound 'A' to 'U'

To change the default 'A' sound of any of the consonantal characters to 'U', simply place a *garlit* 'dot' or 'stroke' above it. For example, *Indûng Súlat* KA (二) becomes *Anak Súlat* KU (二̣) by placing the *garlit* (ˏ) below it.

Example diagram:

wa	wi	wu	we	wo	wá/wâ	wí/wî	wú/wû

DING ÁNAK NING INDÛNG SÚLAT A I (ل)
Altering the vowel glyph I as the consonant Y

One of the features that make Súlat Kapampángan different from the other indigenous scripts of these islands is the way the vowel glyph I (ل) can alter it in the same manner as the consonant glyph YA (∽) found in Baybayin and the other scripts of the archipelago. Although personally, I think the Kapampángan vowel glyph I (ل) is really the consonant glyph YA acting as a vowel glyph. They actually look very similar especially when the Kapampángan character is written in cursive form. As explained by Fray Alvaro de Benavente (1699) in his *Arte de Lengua Pampanga* and by Zoilo Hilario (1962) in his *Báyung Súnis*, the *Indûng Súlat* or "mother character" vowel I (ل) can be altered with the use of a *garlit* or diacritical mark placed above or below it as well as adding vowel ligatures next to it to produce *Anak Súlat* or offspring characters of the consonant sound Y. For instance the *Indûng Súlat* I (ل) can produce the *Anak Súlat* YI (ل) by placing a *garlit* above it and the *Anak Súlat* YU (ل) by placing the *garlit* below it [Table 8].

ya	yi	yu	ye	yo	yá/yâ	yí/wî	yú/yû
ﻝ	ﻝ	ﻝ	ﻝ	ﻝ	ﻝ	ﻝ	ﻝ

Table 8. The anak kulit or offspring characters of the indung kulit I (ل).

DING ÁNAK NING INDÛNG SÚLAT A U (ν)

Altering the vowel glyph U as the consonant W

Again, one of the unique features of Súlat Kapampángan is the way the vowel glyph U (ν) can be altered in the same manner as the consonant glyph WA (ɔ) found in Baybayin and the other scripts of the archipelago. I personally think that the Kapampángan vowel glyph U (ν) may actually be the consonant glyph WA acting as a vowel glyph. Christopher Miller (2011b) also noted the similarity in shape of the Baybayin WA (ɔ) with Kapampángan U (ν). In Kulitan, WA is usually written by combining the vowels characters U (ν) and A (λ) [Table 9] but surprisingly the vowel character U (ν) stood alone without the vowel A (λ) in the 1621 signature of Doña Isabel Pangisnauan of Mexico (Masíku) [Fig. 21]. Could this be proof that Kapampángan vowel character U may actually be the consonantal character WA?

As explained by Fray Alvaro de Benavente (1699) in his *Arte de Lengua Pampanga* and by Zoilo Hilario (1962) in his Báyung Súnis, the *Indûng Súlat* or "mother character" vowel U (ν) can be altered with the use of a *garlit* or diacritical mark placed above or below it as well as adding vowel ligatures next to it to produce *Anak Súlat* or offspring characters of the consonant sound W. For instance the *Indûng Súlat* U (ν) can produce the *Anak Súlat* WI (ν) by placing a *garlit* above it and the *Anak Súlat* WU (ν) by placing the *garlit* below it [Table 9].

wa	wi	wu	we	wo	wá/wâ	wí/wî	wú/wû
ィλ	·ν	ν·	ィλ·ɔ	ィλν	ィλ·ʒ	·ν·ʒ	νν

Table 9. The anak kulit or offspring characters of the indung kulit U (ν).

PÁMANGANAK NING INDÛNG
SÚLAT KING SIWÁLÂNG 'E'
Changing the default vowel sound 'A' to 'E'

Since the Kapampángan vowel sound 'E' was developed from the monophthongisation of the diphthong 'AI', simply place the whole vowel glyph I (ᜁ) right next to the target consonantal glyph to change its inherent vowel sound 'A' to 'E'. For example, *Indûng Súlat* KA (ᜃ) becomes *Anak Súlat* KE (ᜃᜁ) by placing the vowel character I (ᜁ) right after it.

Example diagram:

indûng súlat	+	*indûng súlat a siuálâ*	=	*anak súlat*
ta	+		=	te
la	+		=	le
ga	+		=	ge

PÁMANGANAK NING INDÛNG
SÚLAT KING SIWÁLÂNG 'O'
Changing the default vowel sound 'A' to 'O'

Since the Kapampángan vowel sound 'O' was developed from the monophthongisation of the diphthong 'AU', simply place the whole vowel glyph U (ν) right next to the target consonantal glyph to change its inherent vowel sound 'A' to 'O'. For example, *Indûng Súlat* KA (≒) becomes *Anak Súlat* KO (≒ν) by placing the vowel character U (ν) right after it.

Example diagram:

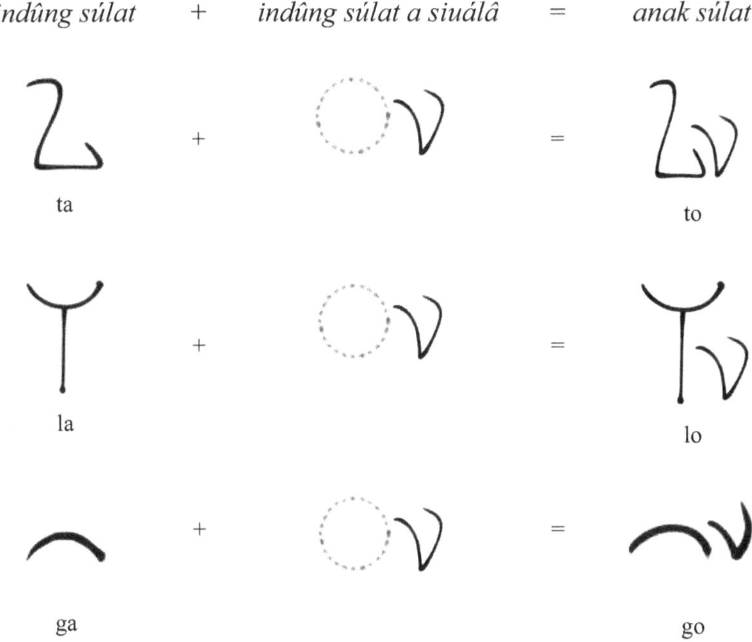

DING KAMBAL SIWÁLÂ
Stress and Accents in Kulitan

The *Kambal Siwálâ* or the lengthening of the vowel sounds in the Kapampángan language indicate the stress emphasis given to one or more syllables in a word. The accents or stress in the Kapampángan language or often lexical in nature. In Kapampángan, there are usually two or more words that are spelled similarly when written in the Latin script. Their meanings are different however depending on which syllable the emphasis falls. Strictly speaking, words having different accents, even if they are spelled the same way, are not the same word (Bachuber, 1952). In the Kapampángan language, a shift in stress may indicate a change in numbers among nouns, a change in tense among verbs, or even a change in the parts of speech (Hilario, 1962, Henson, 1965 and Pangilinan, 2006).

The following classic example comes from Mariano Henson (1965):

masákit	'difficult'	(ADJ.)
másakit	'sick'	(N.)
masakít	'painful'	(ADJ.)

In the Latin script, stress is indicated by the indispensable use of the diacritical marks. A misplacement of these marks could result in a fallacy of accent, or the confusion of one word with another, due to similarity in spelling but with a different reading.

masákit (adjective) 'difficult'	*másakit* (adjective) 'sick'	*masakit* (adjective) 'painful'

KAMBAL SIWÁLÂ 'A'

Lengthening the inherent vowel 'A'

Since all *Indûng Súlat* consonantal glyphs already possess a default vowel sound 'A', simply add the *Indûng Súlat* vowel character A (λ) right after the target glyph. For example, KA (二) becomes medial KÁ (二) or final KÂ (二λ) by placing the vowel character A (λ) right after it.

Example diagram:

indûng súlat	+	*indûng súlat a siuálâ*	=	*anak súlat*
ta				-tá- / -tâ
la				-lá- / lâ
ga				-gá- / -gâ

KAMBAL SIUÁLÂ 'I'

Lengthening the offspring vowel sound 'I'

The vowel sound 'I' of an *Anak Súlat* or offspring character can further be lengthened simply by adding the *Indûng Súlat* vowel character I (ﺝ) right after the target *Anak Súlat* or offspring character. For example, *Anak Súlat* KI (±) gives birth to another *Anak Súlat* ~ the medial KÍ (± ﺝ) or final KÎ (± ﺝ), by placing *Indûng Súlat* vowel character I (ﺝ) right after it.

Example diagram:

anak súlat	+	indûng súlat a siuálâ	=	anak súlat
ti				-tí- / -tî
li				-lí- / -lî
gi				-gí- / -gî

KAMBAL SIUÁLÂ 'U'

Lengthening the offspring vowel sound 'U'

The vowel sound 'U' of an *Anak Súlat* or offspring character can further be lengthened simply by adding the *Indûng Súlat* vowel character U (ꪜ) right after the target *Anak Súlat* or offspring character. For example, *Anak Súlat* KU (꤮) becomes another *Anak Súlat* ~ the medial KÚ (꤮ꪜ) or final KÛ (꤮ꪜꪜ), by placing *Indûng Súlat* vowel character U (ꪜ) right after it.

Example diagram:

anak súlat   +   *indûng súlat a siuálâ*   =   *anak súlat*

tu   +   =   -tú- / -tû

lu   +   =   -lú- / -lû

gu   +   =   -gú- / -gû

PÁMAKAMATÉ SIWÁLÂ
Terminating the default vowel sound

There are two things that actually make Súlat Kapampángan different from all other scripts within the archipelago: First, it is the only script in the archipelago that is traditionally and preferably written vertically top to bottom, left to right, similar to other East Asian scripts. Second, Súlat Kapampángan is also the only script in the archipelago that has managed to create a spelling convention where the final consonant glyph is retained minus its inherent vowel sound 'A' without using a *virama* (vowel killer).This spelling convention has been observed as early as the 17th century based on several Kapampángan signatures from that era (Miller, 2010 and 2011a). While the other indigenous scripts in the archipelago either dropped the coda consonant in the same manner as the Bugis-Makasarese scripts of Indonesia (Miller, 2011a and 2012) or use the *virama* or "vowel killer" in the form of a "cross kudlit" introduced by the Spanish friar Francisco López in 1620 (Marcilla, 1895), the final consonant glyph is written out in full in Súlat Kapampángan but is read without the default vowel sound 'A'.

The only way to appreciate how this is done is by writing Súlat Kapampángan vertically instead of horizontally. To terminate the inherent vowel sound 'A' of any of the consonantal glyphs, simply write the target character next to the one preceding it instead of below it. This will terminate its default vowel sound.

For instance on [Table 10], to terminate the inherent 'A' sound of NA (T) in 'NGANA' simply write NA (T) right next to NGA (ᜅ) instead of below it. This will terminate the default 'A' sound of NA (T), creating the syllable 'NGAN'.

To terminate the inherent 'A' sound of NGA (〰) in the word 'SANGA', simply write NGA (〰) right next to SA (ك) instead of below it. This will terminate the default 'A' sound of NGA (〰), creating the syllable 'SANG'.

To terminate the inherent 'A' sound of SA (ك) in the word 'BUSA', simply write SA (ك) right next to the *anak súlat* BU (O) instead of below it. This will terminate the default 'A' sound of SA (ك), creating the syllable 'BUS'.

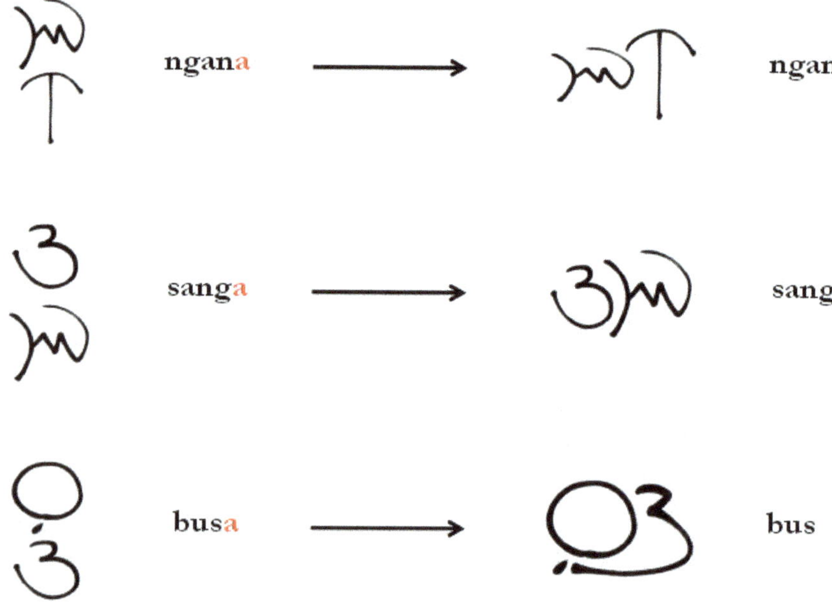

Table 10. Terminating the inherent vowel sound 'A'.

BINÚKUD
Exception to the Rules

One linguist once commented that the Kapampángan language is quite a headache to study because of its complicated and conflicting grammar rules. The language is clearly a reflection of the people's mind and temperament. Like the people themselves, the Kapampángan language creates rules only to break them. Clearly *Kulitan* faithfully reflects the language it represents by creating a number of exceptions to the rules of writing. Normally people write Kulitan as the words are pronounced, a number of exceptions have been made in writing the indigenous names of persons and places, the cross-referent pronouns, and the prefix for negation.

LAGIÛ

Indigenous Surnames and Toponyms

Although *Kulitan* is normally written as it is pronounced, it has a very peculiar rule when it comes to writing indigenous proper nouns. The root word is always spelled out. Therefore, proper nouns are not always written as they are pronounced. Proper nouns are also always separated by two diagonal slashes // before and after them [See the figure embedded in the *Taguláling* at the beginning of this book]. However this rule is not applicable for foreign words or names written in Kulitan.

For instance '*Kapampángan*' is never written as KA-PAM-PA-NGAN but always as KA-PANG-PANG-AN, where the root word *pangpang* or 'river bank' is clearly written [Fig. 40]. The Kapampángan occupational surnames that begin with the prefix MAN- are also not written as they are pronounced but with their root words clearly spelled out. Thus, the surname Maniago is not written as MA-NIA-GO but as MAN-SA-GU with the root word *sagu* or 'horn' clearly written out [Fig. 41] (Bergaño, 1732). The same goes for the surnames Mamangun, Manaloto and Manansala. Mamangun is not written as MA-MA-NGUN but as MAN-BÁ-NGUN where 'BÁ' is a *kambal siuálâ* 'BAA'. The root word is *bángun* means 'to rise up' [Fig. 42] (Bergaño, 1732). The surname Manaloto is written not as MA-NA-LO-TO but as MAN-TA-LAU-TAU [Fig. 43], the root word being *talóto*, which Bergaño (1732) listed down as *talotao* and defined as 'resonance' or 'high sound, like that of a bell or trumpet'. Likewise, the surname Manansala is not written as MA-NAN-SA-LA but as MAN-SAN-SÁ-LÂ [Fig. 44], with the root word *sansálâ* clearly spelled out. Panganiban (1972) defined *sansálâ* as 'prohibition' or 'injunction'. The 'SÁ' and 'LÂ' of *sansálâ* are both *kambal siuálâ* and written as 'SAA' and 'LAA' respectively.

Figure 40. The proper noun Kapampángan is written as KA-PANG-PANG-AN with the root word pangpang clearly spelled out and not KA-PAM-PA-NGAN as it is pronounced.

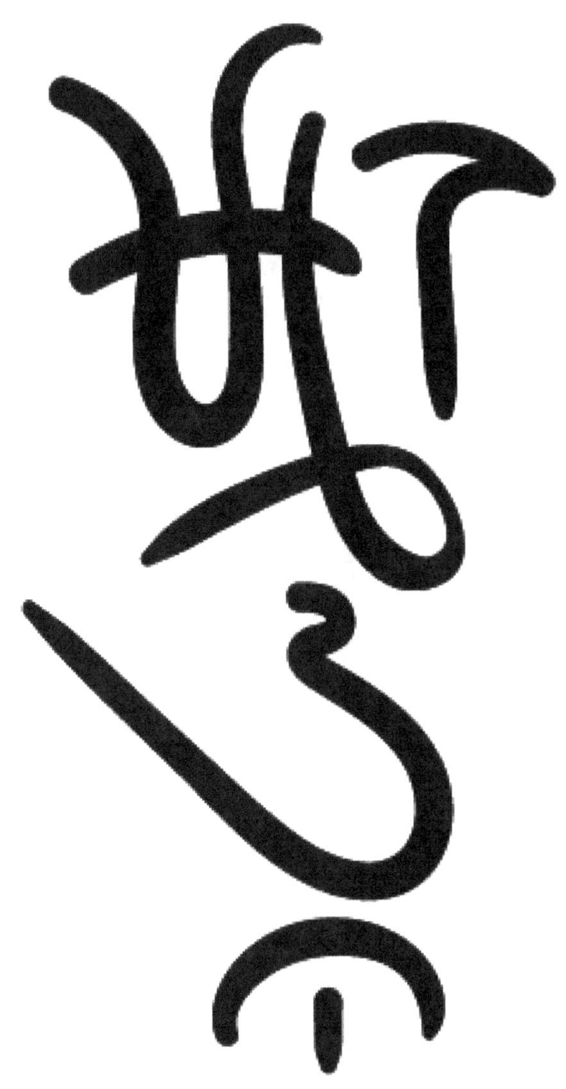

Figure 41. The Kapampángan surname Maniago written as MAN–SA–GU with the root word sagu or 'horn' clearly spelled out.

Figure 42. The Kapampángan surname Mamangun written as MAN-BÁ-NGUN with the root word *bángun* which means 'to rise up' clearly written out.

Figure 43. The Kapampángan surname Manaloto written as MAN-TA-LAU-TAU with the root word talóto or talautau which means 'resonance' or 'high sound' clearly written out.

Figure 44. The Kapampángan surname Manansala is not written as MA-NAN-SA-LA but as MAN-SAN-SÁ-LÂ, with the root word sansálâ clearly spelled out.

ALÍLI
Cross-Referent Pronouns

The Kapampángan language has developed a unique grammar feature known as the cross-referent pronouns which do not exist in the other languages of the archipelago. Cross reference is a peculiar development in Kapampángan syntax where the presence of one grammatical category is redundantly signaled by the third person personal pronoun (Del Corro, 1988). Nominative and genitive pronouns, or ergative and absolutive pronouns, are fused together to create new pronouns which can only be found in the Kapampángan language. In Kulitan, these are written not as they are pronounced. Each individual pronoun is spelled out as they are written originally and fused together to form one word. This will distinguish them from other words or syllables that sound the same way but function differently in Kapampángan grammar. See the following diagram.

	+ ya	+ la		+ ya	+ ya
ku	ké	kó	mi	mi ya	mi la
ta	té	tó	tá	tá ya	tá la
mu	mé	mó	yu	yé	yó
na	né	nó	da	dé	dó

Fused Pronoun Chart

É

Negation

In the Kapampángan language, adjectives can be given the opposite meaning, and verbs given the negative form by simply adding the negative particle 'É' before them. For instance, the adjectives *malagû* (beautiful), *malatî* (small) and *matsúra* (ugly) can be negated if the negative particle 'É' is placed before them: *é malagû* (not beautiful), *é malatî* (not small) and *é matsúra* (not ugly). Kapampángan verbs can also be negated in the same manner. The verbs *mámangan* (eating), *mándílû* (taking a bath) and *mátudtud* (sleeping), for instance, can become *é mámangan* (not eating), *é mándílû* (not taking a bath) and *é mátudtud* (not sleeping) just by placing the negative particle 'É' before them.

The negative particle 'É' however, is a contraction of the Kapampángan word *alî*, 'not' and therefore written as such in *Kulitan* and not as the E (⟨⟩), which is a monophthongized form of the diphthong 'AI'.

Example diagram:

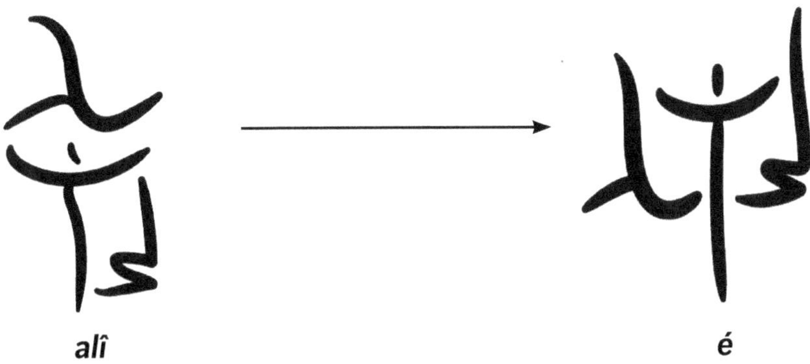

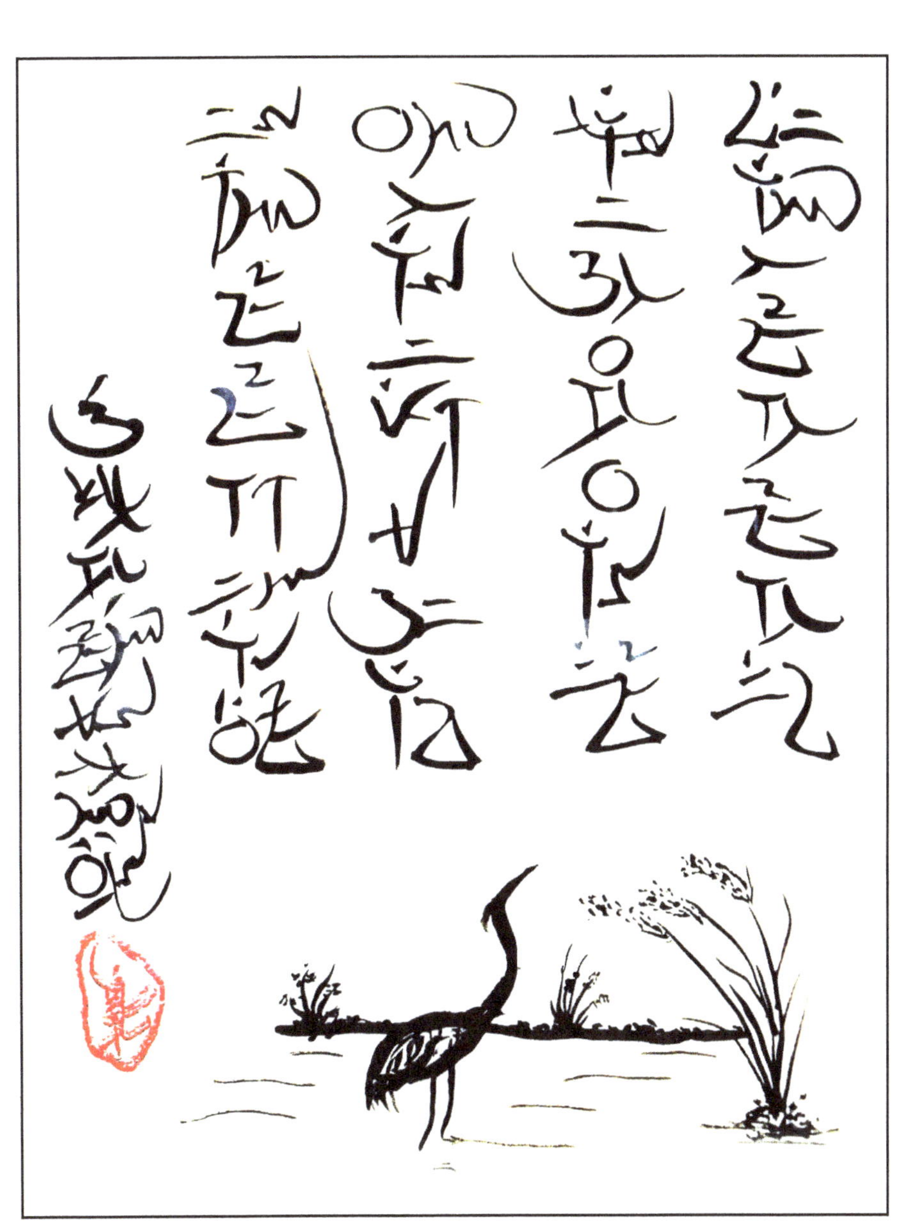

DA

Why Kulitan does not need a separate glyph for RA

First of all, the interchangeability of the /d/ and /r/ sounds when reading Kulitan scripts has more to do with the characteristics of the Kapampángan language itself rather than a writing rule. In Kapampángan, the /d/ sound becomes an /r/ whenever it is preceded and followed by a vowel. This is commonly called as the "vowel-consonant-vowel" pattern or VCV.

For instance, the /d/ sound in the word DAYÛ 'distance' is naturally sounded as /r/ in MÁRAYÛ 'far' because it has lost its initial position and is likewise sandwiched by two vowels (VCV pattern). This also explains why the Spanish word "adobo" is pronounced in Kapampángan as /ʌrɔ:bʊ/ with an /r/ and not with a /d/.

The /d/ sound is retained, however, when in it is in either <u>initial</u> or <u>final</u> position. In the words DAYÛ 'distance' and DÁTANG 'to come,' the /d/ sound is retained because they are placed in the initial position. This also explains why Kapampángans call individuals named Román as Duman.

In the final position, the /d/ sound is also retained, like in the words TÁWAD 'pardon, bargain or forgiveness' and BÁYAD 'payment.'

The words ADDUÂ 'two' and KALADDUA 'soul' are always written with a double D in both Kulitan and the Roman script (Bergaño, 1732 & 1860) so as to retain their /d/ sound [Fig. 45 & 46]. This spelling convention cancels out the VCV (vowel-consonant-vowel) pattern that automatically turns the /d/ sound into /r/.

Fig. 45. The Kapampángan word ADDUÂ 'two' as it is written in Kulitan.

Fig. 46. The Kapampángan word KALADDUA 'soul' as it is written in Kulitan.

Kapampángans who grew up speaking the language therefore do not need a separate glyph to represent the /r/ sound because they would naturally pronounce the /d/ sound as /r/ when it is preceded and followed by a vowel. Those who have a problem with this are usually those who did not grow up speaking the language, or those who can't help but see Kulitan as they would the Roman script.

PANÁMSIK

The affricate consonants /t͡ʃ/ and /d͡ʒ/

AMSIK. The old folks describe AMSIK as the sound of a drop of water hitting a flat stone. It is similar to the sound of the affricate consonants /t͡ʃ/ and the /d͡ʒ/. It is the sound that Kapampángans make whenever they are exasperated or annoyed. It is produced when the tip of the tongue is placed against the teeth and the top of the tongue is rubbed against the palate. Hence, it is also known as SIWÁLANG KASNUK or the sound one makes when annoyed.

The CHA /t͡ʃʌ/ has always been written as *Anak Súlat* TIA (ᜒᜎ) in Kulitan. It is formed when the *Anak Súlat* TI (ᜒ) is fused with *Indûng Súlat* A (ᜎ).

TI (ᜒ) can also be altered to produce the equivalents of CHU, CHÚ, CHE and CHO [Table xx]. The only problem is in writing CHI. Although the CHI /t͡ʃɪ/ and CHÍ /t͡ʃi/ sounds exist in the Kapampángan language, they are not considered a singular glyph. For instance, the Kapampángan and Hokkien word for the eldest sister, ATCHI (阿姊), is pronounced with a CHI /t͡ʃɪ/, but is often written in Kulitan with CHE /t͡ʃɛ/ as A-TIAI [Figure 47].

For those who would insist in writing ATCHI (阿姊) with a CHI /t͡ʃɪ/ instead of the usual CHE /t͡ʃɛ/, then it can only be written as A-T/Yi in Kulitan [Figure 48].

Fig. 47. The Kapampángan and Hokkien word for the eldest sister ATCHI (阿姊),written with CHE /t/ as A-TIAI.

Fig. 48. The Kapampángan and Hokkien word for the eldest sister, ATCHI (阿姊), written as A-T/Yi in Kulitan.

If CHI /t͡ʃɪ/ should be included in the chart [Table xa], it can only be written as a compound glyph [Figure 49].

cha	chá	chi	chí/chî	chu	chú/chû	che	cho

Table xa. Representing affricate consonants CH /t͡ʃ/ in Kulitan.

Fig. 49. CHI /t͡ʃ/ written as a compound rather than a singular glyph.

JA /d͡ʒʌ/ has always been written as *Anak Súlat* DIA (ʒ) in Kulitan. It is formed when the *Anak Súlat* DI (ʒ) is fused with *Indûng Súlat* A (λ). DI (ʒ) can also be altered to likewise further give birth to the *Anak Súlat* equivalents of JU, JÚ, JE and JO [Table xb].

160

ja	já	ji	ji/jî	ju	jú/jû	je	jo

Table xb. Representing the affricate consonants J /dʒ/ in Kulitan.

JI /dʒɪ/ and JÍ /dʒi/ has the same issue as CHI /t͡ʃɪ/ and CHÍ /t͡ʃi/ has the when being written in Kulitan. Although the sound can be easily pronounced by native Kapampángan speakers, there are hardly any words that exist with just JI /dʒɪ/ or JÍ /dʒi/ in it.

Could DÍ/DÎ (ζ₫) also be pronounced as JI /dʒɪ/?

It is interesting to note that the Kapampángans and Hiligaynons have the same word for prayer. The difference is that the Hiligaynons pronounce the last syllable as JI /dʒɪ/, while Kapampángans pronounce it with a DÎ /dɪʔ/. The Hiligaynons' word for prayer is "panggadyî," and for the Kapampángans, PANGADDÎ. Fray Diego Bergaño (1732) recorded PAN-GADDÎ as "panggadiy" in his *Vocabulario de la Lengua Pampanga*. This is written in Kulitan as Pa-N/Ga-D/Di-I [Figure 50], where GAD-DÎ is understood to mean 'seat' or 'throne' of the LAKAN 'god-king.' So could DÍ/DÎ /dɪʔ/ (ζ₫) not also be the same as JI /dʒɪ/?

Fig. 50. PANGADDÎ, the Kapampángan word for prayer.

MÉTÉ YA I SIÁBUKUT

Representing the fricative SH /ʃ/ in Kulitan.

Even if SH /ʃ/ is not a PANAMSIK or SIWÁLANG KASNUK, a separate chapter has not been deemed necessary since it also shares the same patterns and issues as the ones above.

The SH /ʃ/ sound is often described in Kapampángan as *Sásalitsit Pákatiró Pambuk* or 'making a hissing sound with pointed lips.' Compare this to the ordinary /s/ sound that is produced just by baring the teeth.

This sound can be heard in the name of the bird *Siábukut*. It is the main character in the once popular nursery song *Mété ya i Siábukut* or "The *Siábukut* bird has died." People tend to write the name of the bird as "siábukut" or "shábukut" in the Roman script. In Kulitan however, the first syllable is written as SIÁ (𑃤).

SHA /ʃʌ/ has always been written as *Anak Súlat* SIA (𑃤) in Kulitan. It is formed when the *Anak Súlat* SI (𑃤) is fused with *Indûng Súlat* A (𑃣). SI (𑃤) can also be altered to likewise further give birth to the *Anak Súlat* equivalents of SHU, SHÚ, SHE and SHO [Table xc].

sha	shá	shi	shí/shî	shu	shú/hû	she	sho

Table xc. Representing the affricate consonants SH /ʃ/ in Kulitan.

PÁMÍLANG
Numerals

It would seem that Kapampángans quickly adopted the Hindu-Arabic numerals from the Spaniards even before they adopted their Roman alphabets. When Kulitan was being passed down in the 20th century, several writers were already using the modern day Hindu-Arabic numerals side by side with Kulitan, perhaps due to their uniformity. Among the conservatives, each family seem to have its own distinct version.

Many of them use the first two consonantal glyphs GA and KA for the numerals 1 and 2 (*see* Image A). Numeral 3 is often called TULUNG-GÁLUS 'three scratches,' a reference to the Kulitan glyph GA stacked together 3 times. In a way they also look similar to the first three Chinese numerals 一, 二, and 三. When etched or written continuously, Kapampángan numerals 2 and 3 look similar to their modern-day Hindu-Arabic counterpart (*see* Image B). Stylized versions of these line etchings were probably created so as not to confuse the numerals with the glyphs GA and KA (*see* Image C).

Another tradition shows the first three numerals as vertical lines (*see* Image D). These vertical lines are said to represent harvested rice stalks ~ KATANGKÉ 'single rice stalk,' KAKÁSÎ 'partners,' and TALÁTAG 'aligned troops.' Then numeral 4 represents KABIGKIS or KASÍBUG, which is harvested rice stalks bundled together. Numeral 5 represents MANDÁLÂ or bundled rice stalks arranged in certain formation.

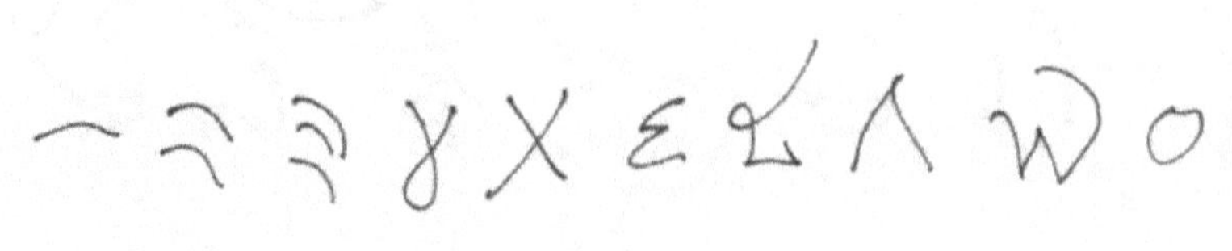

Image A. Notice numerals 1 and 2 are similar to the first two consonantal glyphs in Kulitan, GA and KA. Numerals 1, 2 and 3 also look similar to their Chinese counterpart.

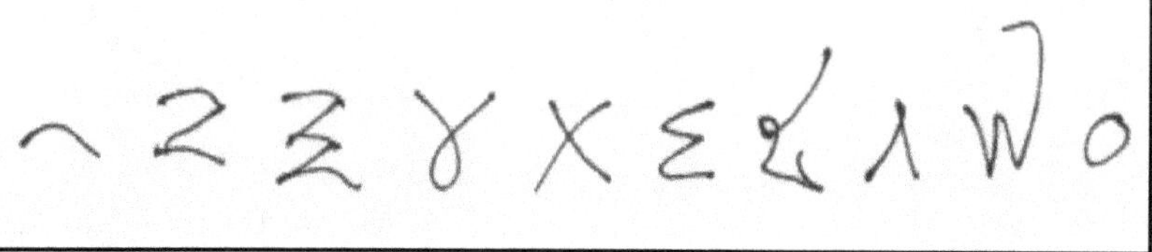

Image B. This is basically the same as Image A, except that numerals 2 and 3 look similar to their Hindu-Arabic counterparts when they are etched continuously.

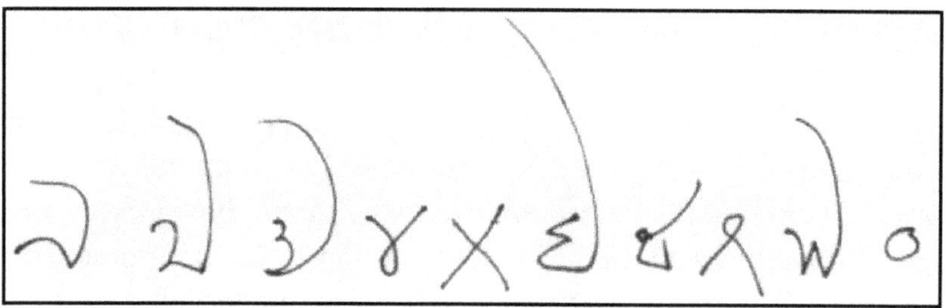

Image C. This is a more stylized variant of basically the same numerals in Image A and B.

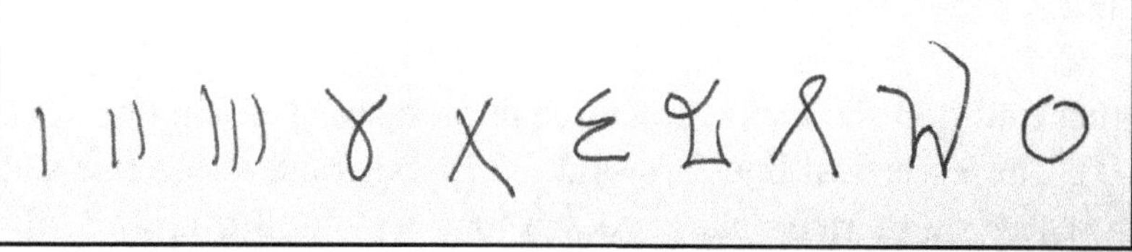

Image D. Shows Kapampángan numerals 1, 2, 3 as vertical lines. They are said to represent rice stalks ~ KATANGKÉ 'single rice stalk,' KAKÁSÎ 'partners,' and TALÁTAG 'aligned troops.' Then numeral 4 represents KABIGKIS or KASÍBUG, which is harvested rice stalks bundled together. Numeral 5 represents MANDÁLÂ or bundled rice stalks arranged in certain formation.

Using Kapampángan numerals is quite easy. Since they possess ALÁYA or zero (0), writing them is similar to writing modern-day Hindu-Arabic numerals [Table 11]. Take note that the 0 numeral is also known as SINGSING 'ring' for obvious reasons. It can be also easily confused with the glyph for BA.

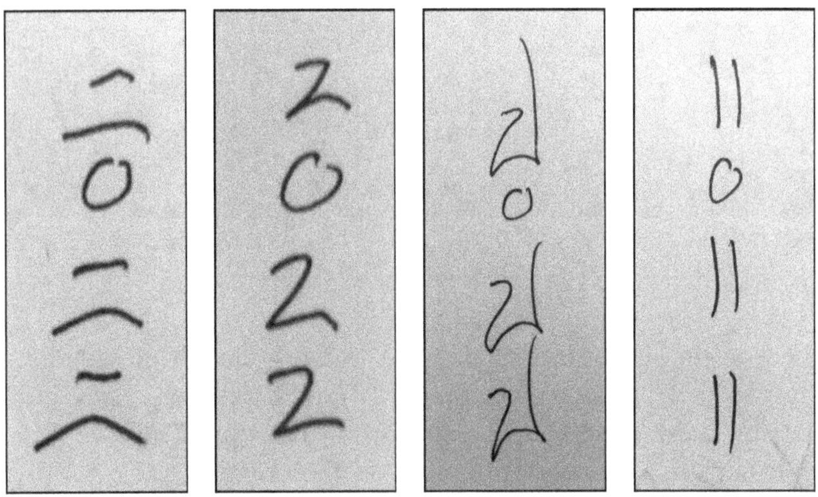

Table 11. Writing the year 2022 in the indigenous Kapampángan script, using the different variations. Numeral 2 written continuously in the second image B looks uncannily like its Hindu-Arabic counterpart.

A lot of Kulitan instructors tend to forget to teach and pass down these numerals they have been too focused with the written word. They often overlook the fact that numbers are written down too. This is may be a result of Western education where "writing" is often limited to "letters." Written works are called "literature," from the Latin word for "letter." In fact, Latin numerals are also written down as letters. Before the introduction of Hindu-Arabic numerals in Europe in the 10th century C.E., there were no separate symbols for letters and numerals. In Eastern cultures, letters and numerals have always been written side-by-side and part of their literature. This ought to be the same attitude for Kulitan.

An interesting artifact is currently on display at the museum of the parish convent in the Kapampángan town of Minalin. It was part of the old beams that were sawed off during the renovation in the late 1990s and early 2000s (see Image F).

Image F. A photo of the etchings found on a piece of a sawed off beam of the church that is currently on display at the Minalin Church Museum.

Etched on the old beams of the 17th century church of Minalin, the characters were initially thought of as Greek or Latin. They did not make any sense in any of those languages however. They would have been dismissed as mere graffiti if not for their regularity.

If read as Kulitan however, one could see that these are combinations of consonant glyphs and numerals. The character that looks like the Roman letter B or even the German ß might actually Kulitan SA. The two stylized Z might actually be the numeral 2 if not the consonant KA. The characters "oYI" might actually read 140 from right to left and the "x" might actually be the Kapampángan numeral 5. The etchings might actually be codes used by the ANLUÁGÎ or traditional Kapampángan carpenters and shipbuilders, to remember where the beams are placed whenever they decide to move and disassemble a wooden structure.

The etchings might read KA KA 140 5 SA. As a wild guess, it could read, "Kábang Kában 140, Kalimang Salû." The KÁBAN refers to the beams laid lengthwise on the roof, while the SALÛ refers to the ribs or beams laid crosswise. The etchings therefore meant, 140th beam lengthwise on the 5th beam crosswise.

SILUSÍLÛ
Cursive Form

TAYIDTÁYID is the Kapampángan term for cursive writing. It only applies to the Roman script. The cursive form of Kulitan is never considered TAYIDTÁYID 'connected.' In the cursive form of the Roman script, each letter is connected by one continuous stroke in each word. This does not happen in Kulitan. In Kulitan, the glyph are not connected to one another in a single word by a continuous single stroke, but rather, glyphs with more than one stroke are written continuously in a single stroke. Hence, the term used is SILÚSÍLÛ or 'creating loops.'

In Kapampángan, the word SÍLÛ refers to the adjustable loop of rope used at the end of a lasso or a snare trap. SILÚSÍLÛ refers to the loop-like pattern in certain objects. In Kulitan, this can often be seen in the glyphs A (ᜀ) and LA (ᜎ) whenever they are written continuously in a single stroke rather than two [Table 12 & 13].

Table 12. Morphing of the glyph A /^/ from two strokes to a single stroke.

171

LA   LA

Table 13. Morphing of the glyph LA from two strokes to a single stroke.

This habit seemed to have started when brush and paper became the instrument and material for writing instead of the old knife and bamboo.

Older folks claim however that this habit is older than paper and that it began at a time when the TAIKTIK, the bamboo stick used as both stylus and whip, became the favored instrument of writing, and that the favored writing material is the GABUN 'soil' or BALAS 'sand.'

The story goes that the hands of the elders who spent much of their energy whipping hard–to-teach kids became too tired to lift their TAIKTIK off the ground when writing on GABUN, so much so that in writing two-stroke glyphs with one stroke, they formed the loops or SILUSÍLÛ. The grumpy old folks mockingly called these, *sílú ding mangaklak a buntuk,* or the "noose for stupid kids."

Other writers see these SÍLÛ 'loops' as BUKNUL 'knots' and so call these BUKNULBUKNUL.

Súlat king Gabun or "writing on sand" was a common practice when tutoring someone as late as the 1970s when paper was expensive and shops that sell school supplies were uncommon. People from the barrios had to recycle old calendars and SÚPUT 'paper bags' to use as notebooks or travel all the way to the urban centers of Angeles and San Fernando

172

to buy them. The use of recycled SÚPUT as writing materials gave rise to the expression SÚLAT SÓSUÂ. SÓSUÂ came from the Hokkien *tsótsua* 粗 紙, which refers to the thin coarse paper used for making currency that is burned as an offering to the dead. SÚLAT GABUN and SÚLAT SÓSUÂ became synonyms for unreliable contracts and agreements because of the ephemeral nature of the material they were written on.

However, GABUN remains a favored writing material for teaching math and Kulitan, especially in the coastal communities of the province of Pampanga, because it is readily available. Although paper is no longer hard to obtain, it is a difficult to preserve medium in an environment that depends on the tides and often remains flooded for almost half of the year [Fig. 51]

Figure 51. The words *Táwu Bátang 'Person from Bátang'* written in Kulitan as SÚLAT GABUN *'writing on sand'* by Aljun Tolentino of the coastal village of Bátang Anak (Bátang II) in the Municipality of Sasmuan in the Province of Pampanga.

Historically speaking, Kapampángan writer and statesman, Don Zoilo Hilario, was known for his "cursive" Kulitan. He was also said to have written a cursive Baybayin KA on the sun of the "new" Katipunan flags used by the KALIBAPI in 1943. Hand written specimens of Don Zoilo Hilario "cursive" Kulitan were preserved in his unpublished 1942 manuscript, *Báyung Súnis* [Table 14].

Table 14. Specimens of Don Zoilo Hilario's cursive Kulitan glyphs from his 1962 Báyung Súnis.

The SILÚSÍLÛ style of writing often occurs in the *Súlat Núnû*, the stylized form of Kulitan used in writing curses, charms and talismans. Some of these can even be considered TAYIDTÁYID because they tend to connect one glyph to the next in one continuous stroke [Fig. 52].

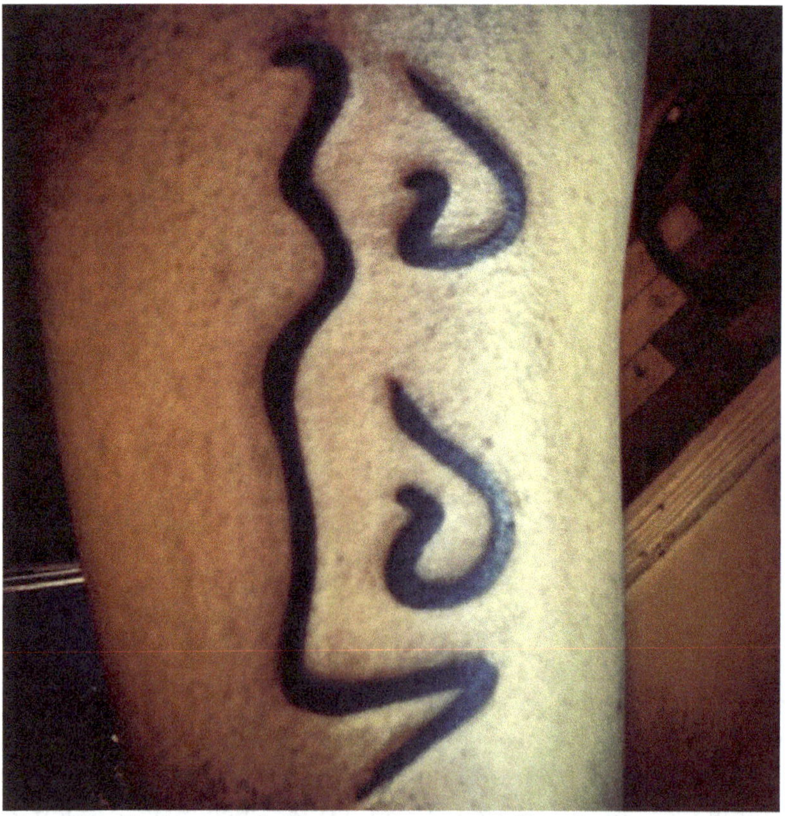

Figure 52. The Kapampángan surname Soto (宋堂) written TAYIDTÁYID as SÚLAT NÚNÛ by Siuálâ ding Meángúbié and tattooed by Speedy Soto on himself in 2013.

PÁTUNG
Writing Direction

One thing that makes Kapampángan people proud of their indigenous script is the fact that it was written vertically top to bottom, right to left, like most traditional East Asian scripts. This is what makes Kulitan unique from all the other indigenous scripts within the archipelago.

There is reason to believe that the other indigenous scripts of the archipelago were written vertically before the coming of the Spaniards. William Marsden (1810) cites an interesting piece from Melchisédech Thévenot's undated *Relation des Philippines par un religieux: traduite d'un manuscrit Espagnol du cabinet de Mons*. Dom Carlo de Pezzo in his *History of Sumatra* that the natives of these islands "used to write from top to bottom, till the Spaniards taught them to write from left to right." Thevenot lived from 1620 to 1692. The original Spanish manuscript he mentioned could be from the same era, if not older. Spanish friar Domingo de Esguerra (1663) wrote in his *Arte de Lengua Bisaya* that the Visayans *"escribir de á bajo hazia arriba"* or that the Visayans used to write vertically from bottom to top. Historian William Henry Scott also wrote that the Tagalog *Baybayin* (1994) can be written in any direction, including vertically.

Sadly, the specimens of the indigenous scripts of these islands available to date, that were preserved during the Spanish colonial era were all written horizontally. These include the Kapampángan specimens from several 17th century signatures provided by Christopher Miller, as mentioned in the previous chapters. This has caused a number of scholars now to doubt the early Spanish observation regarding the vertical direction in writing the indigenous scripts of the archipelago. Paul Morrow (2002) wrote in his *Baybayin* website that the indigenous scripts only appear to be written vertically from bottom to top when the writer carves the letters onto the hard outer bark of strips of bamboo with a sharp object outwards away from the body for safety reasons, in the same manner as the modern Mangyans do today.

A number of scholars tend to agree with him. Also, since most of the known Indian and Indian-inspired *abugida* from the subcontinent to the islands in Southeast Asia have been written horizontally from left to right since ancient times, a number of scholars who reject the vertical direction of the indigenous scripts of the archipelago, to wonder why the writing of these islands should be any different from their Southeast Asian neighbors. This led scholars like Christopher Miller (2012a) and Jean-Paul Potet (2012) to hypothesize that the vertical direction in *Kulitan* or *Súlat Kapampángan* might have been a modern invention.

Kulitan, however, is not the only Indian-inspired *abugida* to be written vertically since ancient times. Siddham (सिद्धं),originally a North Indian script written horizontally from left to right has come to be written vertically from top to bottom, right to left, in Japanese esoteric Buddhism (密教) since its introduction to Japan by Kukai (空海) in 806 C.E. (Pandey, 2012). Siddham, known in Japan as *Bonji* (梵字), is now predominantly used in Japanese esoteric Buddhism to represent the Sanskrit language [Fig. 53]. The official script of the Mongol Empire designed by the Tibetan monk Phagspa for Kublai Khan in 1269 C.E., is another vertical abugida based on the Tibetan script [Fig. 54]. Likewise, the Korean script Hangul, developed in1446 C.E., is another abugida that is originally written vertically (Malaiya, 1997c and Ledyard, 1998). Besides Indian-inspired *abugida*, another script that was originally written horizontally has come to be written vertically is *Sini*, the Arabic script written vertically by Chinese Muslims (Mi Guangjiang, 2007 and 2010) [Fig. 55].

Vertical writing has always been associated with East Asian scripts and often seen as foreign and unnatural by a number of scholars of the indigenous scripts of the archipelago. If this is the case, then it is not far-fetched that the Kapampángan people, as part of the Kingdom of Luzon, learned it from the Chinese and Japanese with whom they

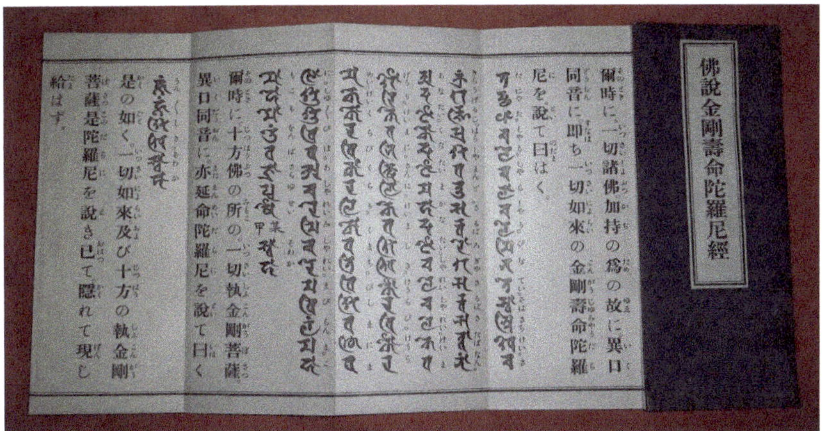

Figure 53. The Tathagatha Vajrayusai Dharani (佛說一切如來金剛壽命陀羅尼) written vertically in Japanese style Siddham from the Tathagatha Vajrayusai Dharani Sutra (佛說一切如來金剛壽命 陀羅尼経) given to me by Alvi Baldomero.

Figure 54. The gravestone of Yáng Wēngshě (楊翁舍) written in Phagspa script, an Indian-inspired script written vertically, dated 1314 from Quanzhou, China (West, 2006b).

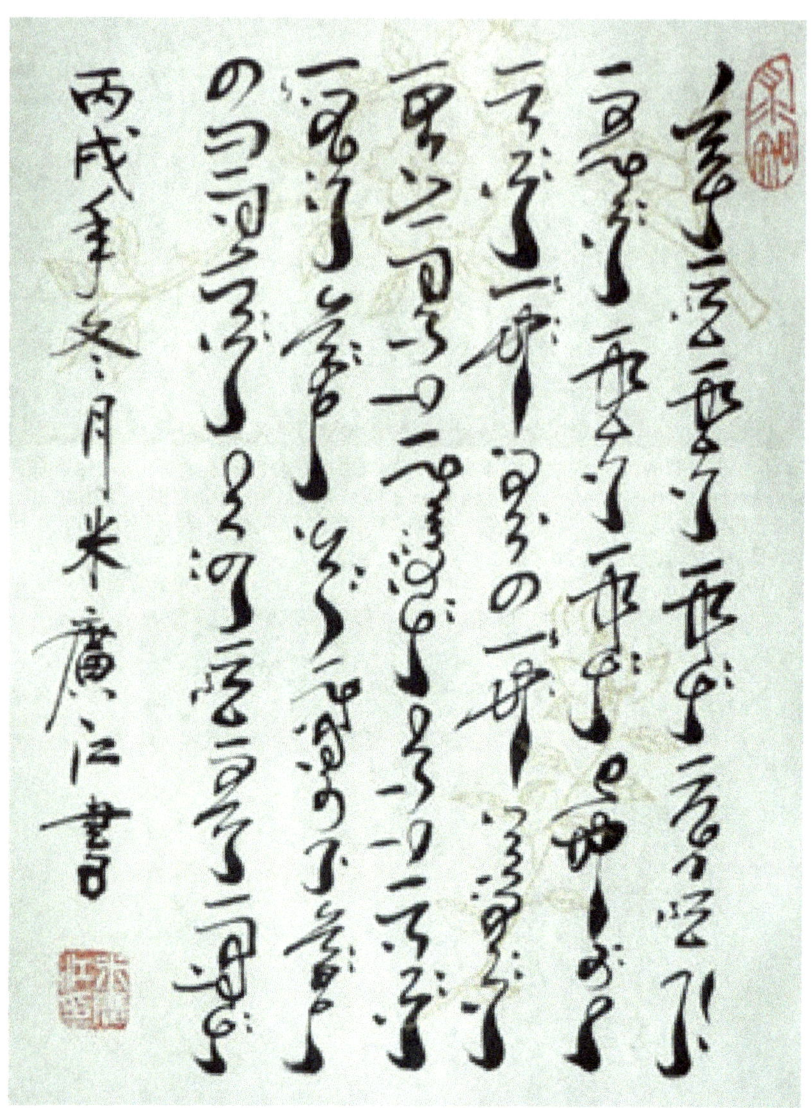

Figure 55. The Sūratul-Fātihah (سورة الفاتحة) or the opening chapter of the Qur'an, written in Sini by Hajji Noor Deen Mi Guangjiang in 2006.

had strong commercial relationships in the mid-16th century. In fact, the traders thought to be Chinese, that traded all over Southeast Asia around that time, were actually merchants from the Kingdom of Luzon (San Agustin, 1699). Since the mid-1500s, the Ming Dynasty closed its doors to foreign trade and forbade its citizens from going outside China except to the Kingdom of Luzon (Wade, 2005). This is the reason why the Kingdom of Luzon became rich in the China trade around this

180

time and why the Japanese merchants that moved their business to her shores became powerful merchants back home. Among them was the 16th century Japanese business tycoon Luzon Sukezaemon (呂宋助左衛門), who changed his surname from Naya (納屋) to Luzon (呂宋) (Barari, 2007). The people of Luzon must have looked and acted like the Chinese to be mistaken for them by their Southeast Asian neighbors. This may even have affected the way their indigenous script was written. In any case, we can only speculate until further research is done and more substantial specimens of ancient Kapampángan writing turn up.

Is vertical writing necessarily an East Asian innovation? Is it not possible for the natives of these islands to develop such a convention on their own, independently of their East Asian neighbors? To push the issue further, could it not be possible that this vertical writing convention was an original development in these islands, and that it was our East Asian neighbors that were influenced by it?

In any case, the vertical direction in writing Kapampángan was never an issue to those who were brought up reading and writing in *Kulitan*. For them, *Súlat Kapampángan* has always been traditionally, and preferably, written vertically top to bottom right to left. They find the questions of outsiders about this to be equally puzzling and ludicrous, to a point.

Folklore tells us that *Súlat Kapampángan* is a gift from the Kapampángan sun god Ápûng Sínukuan, and that the top to bottom and right to left direction is as natural as the movement of the sun to which they offer *pasingtábî*, or homage. As narrated in the verse at the beginning of the book [Fig.1], the vertical direction symbolizes the sun's rays reaching down to earth from the heavens, while the right to left direction stands for the rising of the sun in the East and its setting in the West. The East is always at one's right side whenever one faces the North Star, *Tálâng Úgut*.

Those who reject the vertical orientation of *Kulitan* often cite 17th century Kapampángan signatures that were written horizontally as evidence in their favor, but it is most likely that the horizontal orientation of these signatures are nothing more but a reflection of Spanish influence as mentioned by Thevenot in his *Relation*.

As explained in preceding chapters describing how to terminate the inherent vowel sound, this spelling convention only makes sense if the whole text is written vertically. Trailing consonants can be easily determined by readers when a single word or name is written horizontally as in the case of the 17th century Kapampángan signatures. The case is different however when reading an entire phrase or sentence. Trailing consonants can only distinguished in whole sentences or phrases when written vertically. Take the Kapampángan sentence, "*Méngan yang manuk*" (He ate chicken.), for instance. The trailing consonants are difficult to distinguish when written horizontally [Fig. 56]. This is how this text appears to those who can read Kulitan: 'MA-I-NGA-NA-I-A-NGA-MA-NU-KA'. It does not make any sense in the Kapampángan language.

Figure 56. The Kapampángan sentence "Méngan yang manuk" (He ate chicken) written horizontally. Notice how difficult it is to distinguish the trailing conso-nants. Kulitan experts read this as 'MA-I-NGA-NA-I-A-NGA-MA-NU-KA' if written this way.

The case is different, however, when the whole sentence is written vertically in syllable blocks, as they are supposed to be written [Fig. 57]. All of the trailing consonants can readily be seen, and therefore read accordingly, without their inherent vowel sounds. The whole sentence makes perfect sense when written this way.

To close the matter, for Kapampángans, *Kulitan* is written vertically simply because it makes sense that way. Imagine how confusing it would be if the Kapampángan song *Atin Ku Pûng Singsing* is written horizontally like Baybayin, and not vertically, in syllable blocks, as in this example [Fig. 58].

Figure 57. The Kapampángan sentence "Méngan yang manuk" (He ate chicken) written vertically. Notice how easy it is to read the whole sentence as it is spoken. Every every trailing consonant and vowel conjuncts can be easily distinguished since they are arranged in syllable blocks.

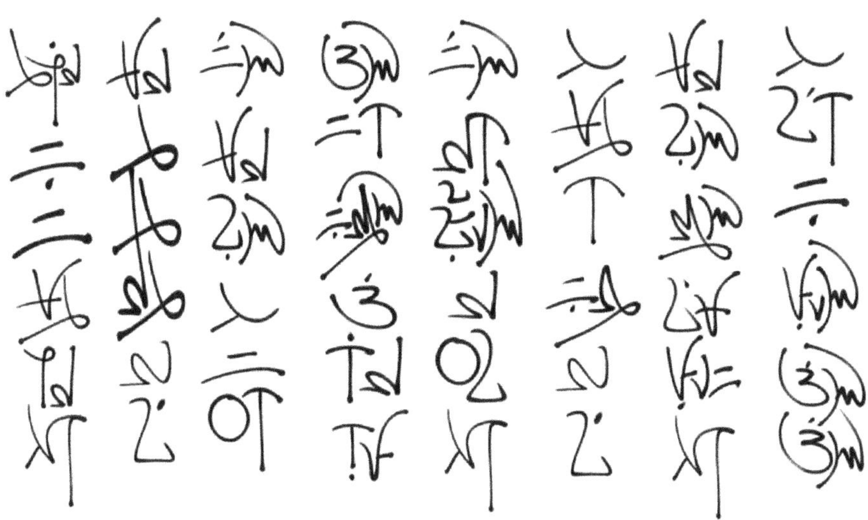

Figure 58. The traditional Kapampángan basultû or coded song Atin Ku Pûng Singsing written vertically top to bottom left to right by Siuálâ ding Meángûbié (Michael Raymon M. Pangilinan).

BÁYUNG SÚLÎ
Innovations

This is practically a totally new chapter. The old chapter from the first edition has been attacked non-stop by traditionalists that they named it *Báyung Málî* 'new mutants' instead of *Báyung Súlî*. Eventually, many of the proposed innovations were rejected by both old and new writers alike, except for a few that shall be taken into consideration here.

The Kapampángan people have been exposed to different languages and cultures and have adopted many foreign words into their native lexicon, particularly from Sanskrit and Minnan Chinese (閩南語) or what is popularly known as Hokkien (福建話). Many words from these languages, such as the Kapampángan words DAMLÂ 'noble purpose' and KALMÂ 'fate' from Sanskrit *dharma* and *karma*, and Kapampángan terms of endearment INGKUNG 'maternal grandfather' and ATCHI 'eldest sister' from Hokchow [閩東語] *ngiêng-gŭng* [外公] and Hokkien *a-chí* [阿姉], were thought to be indigenous by native Kapampángan speakers. Traditional writers have no problem in writing these words in Kulitan.

The resistance, however, can still be felt towards the acceptance and the writing of Spanish and English loanwords to Kulitan. This is perhaps due to the long periods of conflict and resistance during the colonial era where Kulitan was used as the script of those who rejected foreign influences and opposed foreign rule.

For instance, the Spanish loanwords *kurus* 'cross' and *lamesa* 'table' can be found in the second stanza of the iconic Kapampángan song *Atin ku pung Singsing*, yet these words were not written in Kulitan but as drawings or symbols [Fig. 59].

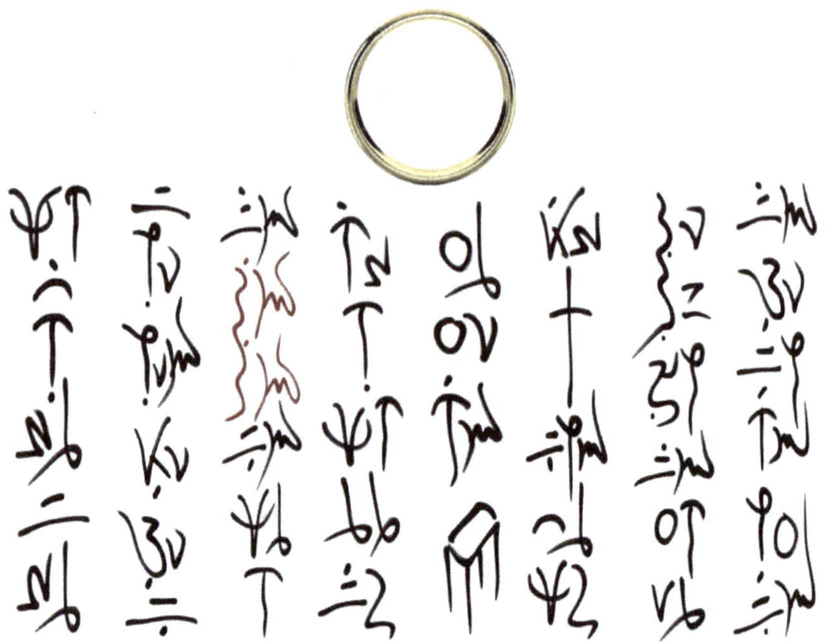

Figure 59. The second stanza of Atin ku pung Singsing *where* kurus *'cross' and* lamesa *'table' are not written in Kulitan.*

Sadly in this era, not every Kapampángan was brought up in a traditional household full of resentment towards their former colonial masters. Not every Kapampángan was brought up in folklore and the old traditions, nor in reading the classics and in polishing their Kapampángan vocabulary.

The vocabulary of the common Kapampángan individual today is peppered with English and Tagalog lexicon. He or she would also be exposed to Japanese or Korean. Many others would have lived abroad and have exposed themselves not only to English but also to Arabic, French, German, Russian and many other languages. These can be evidenced by the new names Kapampángan children have. Rather than the usual American names or the traditional Spanish ones, you would hear names that sound so alien that you begin to wonder what languages they were actually derived from.

Since the Kapampángan language can now accommodate a variety of sounds that it can pronounce due to the people's exposure to foreign languages and the influx of foreign vocabularies into their language, a number of the new Kulitan writers are beginning to feel the limitations of writing in Kulitan.

This was never a problem among Kulitan writers since traditionally there was a PANGÍLIN 'taboo' in using the indigenous script to write foreign words. However, as the number of Kulitan writers continued to grow, a number of young Kulitan writers began to question this taboo.

In 2008, Kulitan writers became divided between the traditionalists and the non-traditionalists. Traditionalists argue that writing foreign words in Kulitan would defile its perceived sanctity and debase its unspoken mystical nature. The non-traditionalists want to see a practical use for Kulitan and free it from its marginal role among artists and mystics. They argue that unless Kulitan adapts and quickly becomes popular, it is destined to die out ahead of the endangered Kapampángan language it represents. A number of them proposed certain innovations among fellow experts that would accommodate the writing of new and foreign words that made their way into the Kapampángan vocabulary.

On the Issue of Consonant Clusters

The Kapampángan language normally follows a syllable pattern wherein consonants never cluster, but are always spaced by vowels (Del Corro, 2008). For example, in the initial consonant cluster [cr-] for the Spanish word *cruz*, Kapampángans tend to insert a vowel in-between so that they can pronounce it. The resulting word is the Kapampánganized / kurus/.

Similarly, Kapampángans also always tend to insert vowels in the consonant clusters [tr-] and [-xt-] in the English words "truck" and "sixty" respectively. Hence, you will hear old Kapampángans saying /tarak/, instead of "truck" and /síkisíti/ instead of "sixty." Kulitan naturally mirrors this syllable pattern in the Kapampángan language.

Surprisingly though, Kapampángans speakers do not find any difficulty in pronouncing final consonant clusters. The English words 'bark', 'bond' and 'tart' are pronounced easily, even without inserting any vowels between the consonant clusters /rk/, /nd/ and /rt/.

Even traditionalist find it easy to write the English names Mark, Bart and Max ('x' as consonant cluster /ks/) in Kulitan by simply following the rules in writing final consonants without their inherent vowel sound A /ʌ/ Table 15]. In this case however, two consonantal glyphs stacked over the other are placed next to the preceding glyph.

indûng súlat	+	*kinulit*	=	*kinulit*
ma	+	daka	=	mark
ba	+	data	=	bart
ma	+	kasa	=	max

Table 15. Diagram showing how final consonant clusters in English names are written in Kulitan.

If Kapampángans find no difficulty in pronouncing and writing final consonant clusters in Kulitan, pronouncing and writing initial consonant clusters remain a challenge. For instance, the English word 'start' is pronounced as 'is-tart' following the syllable pattern of the Kapampángans language. If it could be written in Kulitan, it would be written as thus, following the syllable pattern.

The surname 'Cruz' and first name 'Chris' have always been pronounced as /ku-rus/ and /ki-ris/. The younger generation however no longer finds it challenging to articulate these foreign names. They now find it easy to pronounce 'krus' and 'kris' as one syllable without inserting any vowels in between the consonant cluster [kr-].

Since many of the new Kulitan writers belong to this generation, they wanted to write these names as they pronounce them. This is why they find the indigenous Kapampángans script wanting. Although writing final consonant clusters fit naturally with the traditional rules, the writing of initial consonant clusters would require a new convention and possible innovation.

In the first edition of this book, the Ágúman Súlat Kapampángan suggested the creation of consonant conjuncts to represent the initial consonant clusters, such as adding the stem [ᔓ] taken from the lower part of consonantal glyph DA [ᕼ] and then attaching it to the *Indung Súlat* glyphs.

To create the initial /kr/ in the name Kris for instance, they suggested attaching the stem [ᔓ] taken from the lower part of consonantal glyph DA [ᕼ] below the glyph KA [ᐃ] and form the *Báyung Súling* glyph KRA [ᔔ]. They suggested the same thing for the initial consonant clusters [kl-], [pl-] and [bl-] for the Spanish loan words "klási," "plánu," and "blánku" and took stems from the Indung Súlat glyph LA.

Ironically, no one accepted nor adopted these suggested innovations, not even by the members of the Ágúman Súlat Kapampángan. By 2019, the members of the Ágúman Súlat Kapampángan became conservative and traditionalist themselves and looked at these suggestions recorded in the first edition with aversion. The tables with several of these examples were no longer included in this edition.

The writing of initial consonant clusters will remain an issue. Perhaps in future editions a better solution would have been found if necessary.

Likewise, the suggestion of the Ágúman Súlat Kapampángan to create entirely new glyphs for CHA /t͡ʃʌ/, JA /d͡ʒʌ/ and SHA /ʃʌ/ have been rejected by everyone, including by those who suggested it. These sounds can still be written just fine in the old traditional way.

"*Ót larínan mé ing é naman sirâ* (Why fix something that is not even broken)," Kulitan writer Justin Calmâ Lacson of Angeles City once queried. If the old way works just fine, why invent a new one?

Unanimously, old and new writers, traditionalists and non-traditionalists alike, have agreed that the usual way works just fine in representing CHA /t͡ʃʌ/, JA /dʒʌ/ and SHA /ʃʌ/. The tables from the first edition representing these have been removed upon their suggestion. For in-depth discussions on the traditional way of representing CHA /t͡ʃʌ/, JA /dʒʌ/ and SHA /ʃʌ/, read the new chapter entitled PÁNAMSIK in this new edition.

It would seem that not all of the proposed innovations have been rejected. For instance, the proposed glyph for the sounds /x/ and /z/ has been tried and accepted by other writers, including the author of this book. The new glyph XA [ろ] was formed with the fusion of the glyphs KA [二] and SA [ろ], while the new glyph ZA [ろ] was formed with the fusion of the glyphs DA [ろ] and SA [ろ] [Table 16].

XA   ZA

Table 16. The new glyphs XA [ろ] and ZA [ろ].

These new glyphs however remain limited to writing foreign names favored by the new Kapampángan generation. They are also used mainly in the initial and final position of such names, like in the end of [lex] in the name Alex or in the beginning of names like Xander or Xandrea [Fig. 60]. The old rule applies if the sounds /x/ and /z/ appear in medial position. For instance, the /z/ in the name Byzyntryx would be written as [ds], where the preceding syllable would be written as [bid] that ends with the glyph DA [ ] and the succeeding syllable, [sint] would begin with the glyph SA [ ]. The [ryx] would be written as [rix] that ends with the proposed glyph XA [ ].

Figure 60. The new glyph XA ( ) tattooed by Marlon Jon Maristela on Xandrea Castro in 2012.

PÁMAGLÁBUNG

DEVELOPMENT

KABAYANGNAN
Youth Activism

Although the use of Kulitan remains emblematic at most, it is no longer limited to signatures, tattoos and logos. In the last ten years since the first edition of this book was published, there seems to be a serious effort to learn, teach and promote the indigenous Kapampángan script. Several instructional blogs and videos have appeared online. Online and face-to-face Kulitan workshops and tutorials are being advertised regularly. There is even a learn Kulitan mobile phone application that can be downloaded for free on the App Store for iPhones and Google Play Store for Android mobile phones. This application helps you learn how to read and write Kulitan even without a book or a real-life human instructor. This was designed by a young tech graduate from the University of the Philippines in Los Baños, Laguna, Keith Liam Manaloto of Angeles City in 2019 [Fig. 61].

Figure 61. The "Learn Kulitan" mobile phone application designed by Keith Liam Manaloto of Angeles City in 2019.

Credit all this development to the Kapampángan youth, a growing number of which have become cultural activists and advocates who began to question the truth about their ethnicity and sought answers about their cultural heritage and identity. They are responsible for expanding Kulitan's domains and making it more visible and accessible to the public.

Many of them have found the indigenous Kapampángan script as a powerful living relic of their cultural heritage and a very tangible symbol of their ethnic Kapampángan identity. The book on Kulitan served as their anchor to a cultural identity that they thought they have forever lost. Those who have read it attests that the book helped them reclaim their long buried Kapampángan Self and finally gave them back their *Damlâ*, their purpose and sense of direction.

Figure 62. Kapampángan descendants from the former Kapampángan enclave of Tungdû (Tondo), now part of the city of Ménílâ (Manila), wearing Kulitan shirts brushed by Taram Kalis (Eugene David Ngo) of Angeles City. Despite becoming Tagalog-speakers for generations, they still proudly consider themselves ethnic Kapampángans.

Kapampángan language and culture activism seems to be a natural thing for many Kapampángans who decided to leave home to study outside of *Indûng Kapampángan*, their Kapampángan homeland. They begin to miss their friends and families, but most especially the taste of their mother's cooking. Even hearing and speaking their *Amánung Sísuan*, their native Kapampángan language, which they have learned to look down in school as just a mere dispensable provincial dialect, becomes a precious experience. Questions begin to form in their minds regarding their ethnicity and identity. They begin to doubt the teachings at school that their language is a mere insignificant rural dialect that can be discarded for the sake of patriotism and nation building, that they ought to only use and favor the more dominant national language, Filipino (Tagalog) and its global counterpart, English.

What is more surprising then is the growing number of Kapampángan activism among the youth who never left Indung Kapampángan. In the last few years, Kapampángan activism seem to have become an organic thing among Kapampángan high school students from both public and private schools in the last few years. Not surprisingly, Kulitan writers are at the forefront of these Kapampángan activist groups.

In private schools, a number of students have become radicalized due to the harsh and restrictive language policies that specifically ban the use of the Kapampángan language within their campuses. Students from OB Montessori and Holy Family Academy in Angeles City and Don Bosco Academy in Mabalacat formed their own "underground" Kapampángan organizations and often sent their representatives to the Sídduan ning Kabiasnan Kapampángan (later Sínúpan Singsing: Center for Kapampángan Cultural heritage) for advice and consultation. Some of them later became volunteers at the center, attending several seminars and workshops (Pangilinan, 2021).

In public schools, Kapampángan underground activism exists not only among the students, but also among the teachers. It was said to be a reaction against the dominance of Tagalog a.k.a. Filipino in education and the arrogant posturing of its proponents who were said to belittle Kapampángan language and culture. Ever since Tagalog became the national language called Filipino, anything Tagalog became Filipino. Kapampángan teachers are made to teach Tagalog History as *Kasaysayan* (Filipino History), Tagalog Literature as *Pánitikan* (Filipino Literature) and Tagalog Language as Filipino, a.k.a. *Wikang Pambansa* (national language) and *Sariling Wika* (our own language). Doing anything Tagalog has become a patriotic act, from speaking the language to wearing the required native Tagalog dress, *Barong Tagalog*, on formal occasions.

Astonishingly, this underground public school activism exists in the town of Bakúlud (Bacolor), the old capital of the province of Pampanga once hailed as the "Athens of Pampanga," for being the center of Kapampángan literature and the home of several Kapampángan literary giants like Crissot (Juan Crisostomo Soto), Felix Galura, Mariano Proceso Pabalan y Byron, and Fr. Anselmo Fajardo. Naturally, young Kulitan writers are at the forefront of this Kapampángan activism.

Figure 63. Kulitan writers from the senior high school Humanities class of 2019 at the Don Honorio Ventura State University (DHVSU) in Bakúlud (Bacolor). Kapampángan activism at DHVSU began with the Kulitan writers of the previous year.

Currently, Kapampángan language and culture is under threat from the now dominant language and culture, Tagalog a.k.a. Filipino. This is quite evident in schools, private or public, where the Kapampángan language has been suppressed for generations.

In a country where indigenous knowledge is being buried by a supposedly "more advanced" knowledge adopted from the West, where the history of one's people is being swept aside by the mainstream Manila-

Tagalog narrative, where every indigenous ethnic group is forced to become Filipino and sacrifice their own languages and cultures for the sake of national unity, the indigenous Kapampángan script, Kulitan, have become an expression of identity and resistance by the defiant Kapampángan youth. `

PANIÚLUNG
Advancement

Kapampángans are highly fortunate that cultural activism is being spearheaded by the youth, many of whom are Kulitan writers. They belong to the generation who know how to effectively use the latest technology in advancing the teaching and learning of Kulitan. Unlike in other cultures where modernization and technology are seen as destroyers of culture, the Kapampángan youth saw technology as an effective tool in saving it.

Most remarkable of these was the "Learn Kulitan" mobile phone application that was designed by Keith Liam Manaloto as part of his college thesis at the University of the Philippines in Los Baños, Laguna in 2019 [Fig. 64]. Kapampángans across the globe have probably downloaded this app thousands of times from the App Store and Google Play Store since it came out in 2019.

Figure 64. The "Learn Kulitan" mobile phone application designed by Keith Liam Manaloto of Angeles City in 2019.

With the "Learn Kulitan" app, Manaloto also developed his own Kulitan digital fonts that can be downloaded for use in typing Kulitan texts on word processing programs for computers and mobile phones. The only problem is what specific word processing software to use in continuously and conveniently typing Kulitan vertically.

Despite the fact that many Kapampángan cultural activists use Kulitan for actual written communications and no longer limit it to mere emblematic use, the inability to type it by computer or mobile phones can be very frustrating, especially to a young population who prefer to use digital technology for practically everything, from banking and finance, to marketing and trading.

As of date, Kulitan has not yet been encoded in Unicode. This would have made it easy to use in digital word processing. In 2019, Manaloto began coordinating with American software developer and type designer Frederick Brennan in finding ways to encode Kulitan in computer entry. Sadly, no news or development has been received from Brennan since the Corona virus pandemic broke out in 2020.

It was actually Emerson Navarro Camaya of Tarlac, Tarlac who first encoded Kulitan in digital format on BASIC for his IBM personal XT computer when the Windows operating system first came out in 1996. He created the first digital Kulitan fonts with his brother, the Kapampángan activist Edwin Navarro Camaya.

With Camaya's fonts, Kulitan can be typed vertically by creating table columns on Microsoft Word. It was still tedious work since Word isn't really designed for vertical writing. There was also no means to compress each syllable into uniform blocks whenever they contained more than one glyph. It is still entirely different from encoding them in Unicode.

Encoding Kulitan for computer entry has remained elusive due to its vertical writing orientation (Miller, 2011 and Pandey, 2012). A word processing program must be developed for Kulitan, similar to the ones made for writing East Asian scripts vertically. This could be patterned after the programs used specifically in writing Korean Hangul vertically, since this script somewhat similar to alphasyllabaries like Kulitan.

Most, if not all, Kulitan writers do not want to compromise the vertical nature of the indigenous Kapampángan script. They have strongly expressed that they would just endure the inconvenience of writing it by hand and forego the expediency of typing it on the computer and mobile phones if encoding it in Unicode would entail having to sacrifice the distinct vertical orientation in writing the script.

Problems were foreseen if Kulitan were to be written horizontally, particularly the method of terminating final vowel sounds. Vertically, Kulitan is written per syllable block, not so different from Hangul (Miller, 2011). Could this integrity be maintained should Kulitan be written horizontally? How would these syllable blocks be written distinctly if these were to be typed horizontally?

Also, a horizontally written Kulitan might appear no different from the Tagalog Baybayin. Baybayin advocates then could easily claim Kulitan as just another regional variant of the Tagalog script. If the Kapampángan script becomes a mere regional variant of Tagalog, then it would no longer require a separate encoding for computer entry (Miller, 2011).

This will also make it easier for Tagalog script advocates to once again push for the legislation of Baybayin as the national script of the country and force its study and use on everyone in the islands, regardless of their existing writing systems. This would be no different from the legal imposition of the Tagalog language as the national language of the Philippines called Filipino that has for generations marginalized all other languages in the archipelago to the point of endangerment.

At present, the main opposition to the legal imposition of the Tagalog Baybayin as a national script of the Philippines are the passionate writers and advocates of Kulitan, much to the annoyance of Tagalog script advocates.

PÁMITUGMÁTUGMÂ
Kulitan and Social Media

The presence of Kulitan on social media and online blogs in the last decade or so, particularly on Facebook and YouTube, not only attracted the attention of the Kapampángan diaspora across the globe, but also scholars and scripts enthusiasts who are not necessarily Kapampángan. The indigenous Kapampángan script gained a lot of international attention and recognition.

Through social media, Kulitan writers from across the globe found connection and a common ground with which to communicate with other Kulitan writers. It is frustrating therefore that they could not use Kulitan on computer entry and in typing messages on mobile phones.

Unlike Tagalog Baybayin, Kulitan has not yet been encoded in Unicode. At present, Kulitan writers still brush or write their messages by hand, and then scan or photograph them before they can upload them digitally online. It is tedious work, compared to Tagalog Baybayin that can now be typed directly onto one's computers or mobile phones. Still, Kulitan writers are willing to forego the convenience of typing it onto computers and mobile phones so that they can preserve its distinct vertical nature.

This however resulted in best penmanship in both brush and pen ever produced online. Those with the best penmanship in the indigenous script posted online include Jayvie Suasi Aboyme of Apalit [Fig. 65], Allandail Lumanlan Rivera of Mawaque in Mabalacat, and Alfred Íbé Malazza of Arayat. Those with the best brush calligraphy include Raymond Bondoc Figueroa of San Luis [Fig. 66] and Taram Kalis (Eugene David Ngo) of Angeles City.

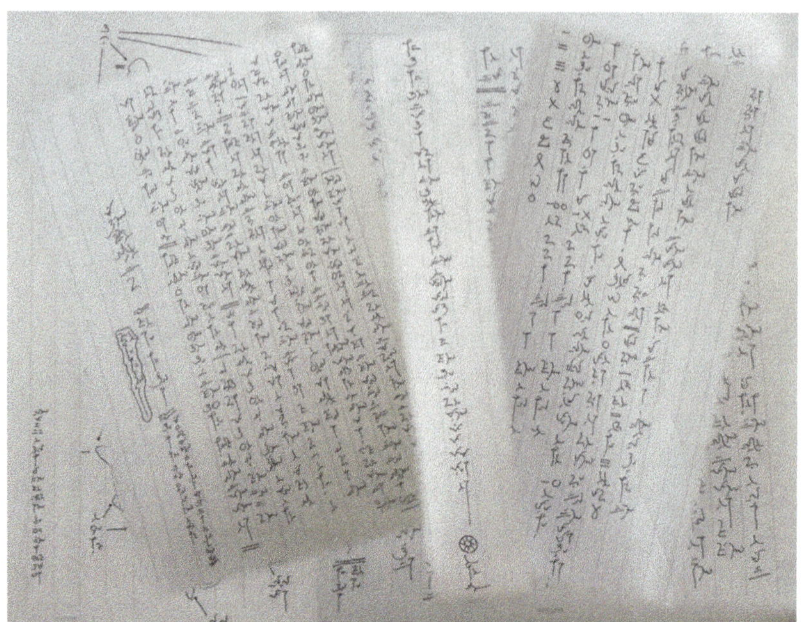

Figure 65. A collection of Kulitan penmanship specimens from Jayvie Sua-si Aboyme of Apalit.

Figure 66. Kulitan brush calligraphy by Raymond Bondoc Figueroa of San Luis, Pampanga.

Aside from Facebook, Jayvie Suasi Aboyme and Allandail Lumanlan Rivera, maintained their own blogsite where they continued to post their Kulitan penmanship and their thoughts about the indigenous Kapampángan script in particular and Kapampángan language and culture in general.

Not to be outdone in posting Kulitan on social media would be the digital graphic artists, like Aljon Medina of San Fernando, John Manuntag of Candaba, Aljun Tolentíno of Sasmuan, Kelvin Dimalanta of Floridablanca, Marlo (Mark Laurenz) Garcia of Mabalacat, Marlon Macabanti and Ian Manalo Saléngâ of Angeles City.

This inability to input Kulitan digitally on to computers in order to communicate and exchange ideas has further developed Kulitan as a visual art form that is beyond the traditional brush and ink calligraphy. Perhaps the leading proponent in this is Norman Philip Pecjo Tiotucio of Angeles City and the members of the Ágúman Kalalangan Súlat Kapampángan (AGKAS). Not to be left behind are the independent visual artists and Kulitan writers Lloyd Dacayanan of Sápangbatu, Ágí ning Aldo (Dodgie Aguinaldo) of Mabalacat, Jing Torno and Lucio Sison of Angeles City.

More than thirty years ago, long before social media, Kapampángan visual artists like Pax Pineda, Edille Paras, Ronnie Táyag, Gelo Espiritu and Tétâ (Lorina Táyag Capitulo) of the Angeles-based Pampanga Arts Guild (PAG), have already experimented with the indigenous Kapampángan script and have incorporated them in their artwork. These however were sporadic and not regular since they were not borne out of the necessity to communicate online.

PÁMANÚLID
Designing a Kulitan-based Orthography

Kevin Bätscher, a linguist from the University of Hawaii, noticed that the Kapampángan language makes a phonemic distinction between long and short vowels. These were accurately represented in Kulitan (Pangilinan, 2015) but never in the Roman script.

For instance, a number of Kapampángan words are written exactly the same way in the Roman script but are pronounced differently. The most classic comparison are the words MASAKIT (painful), MÁSAKIT (sick) and MASÁKIT (difficult) [Table 20]. Words written in the same way but pronounced differently are not the same words. In the example below,

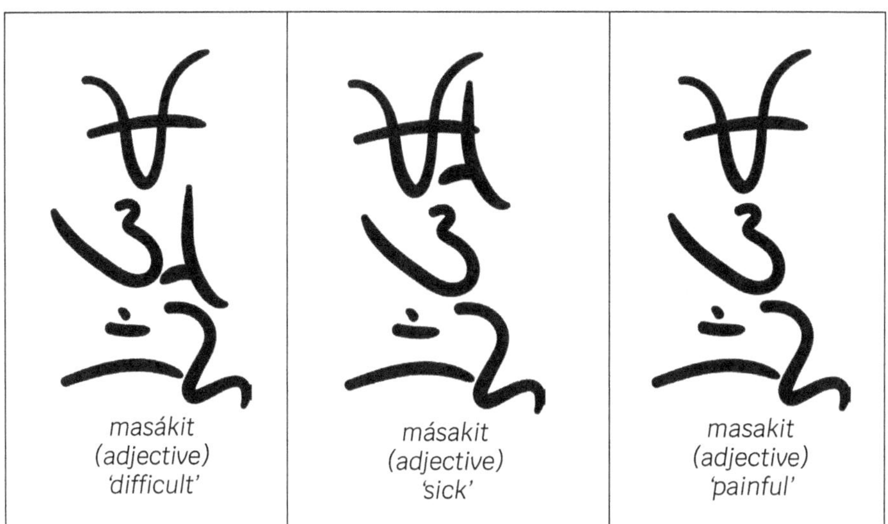

Table 20. The three words above are often misread in Romanized Kapampángan writing, especially when the necessary diacritical marks are misplaced or omitted. In Kulitan, the difference between these words is obviously evident.

a diacritical mark placed above the long vowel helped distinguish the difference. This is a novelty for Kapampángan speakers, most of whom were never taught to read and write their own language in school due to decades of suppression.

Likewise, none of the existing literature and dictionaries, with the exception of Venancio Samson's, do not reflect this phonemic distinction. This does not help the increasing number of people who wanted to learn the Kapampángan language, including Bätscher.

Fortunately, Bätscher learned Kulitan. This helped him determine this phonemic distinction that is currently not evident in the existing orthography in the Roman script.

At a lecture held in 2019, the Sínúpan Singsing: Center for Kapampángan Cultural Heritage in Angeles City, Bätscher made the following conclusion in his lecture entitled "What Kulitan can teach us about Kapampángan Phonology:"

1. Kulitan reliably represents the phonemic distinctions of Kapampángan;

2. Kulitan is perfectly concise, using the minimal number of required symbols aside from epenthetic glides;

3. Kulitan has the oldest writing tradition for Kapampángan;

4. Kulitan is unique to Kapampángan, setting it apart from competing languages;

5. The one major drawback of Kulitan is that it can't be typed (yet);

6. Romanization of Kapampángan can simply follow Kulitan as standard.

As for the last statement, the Ágúman Sínúpan Singsing, Inc., with Bätscher's help, designed a more accurate Kulitan-based orthography for Kapampángan being written in the Roman script which has been included as an appendix in this current edition. This was also supposed to be the official orthography in the Implementing Rules and Regulations of the Local Language Code of Angeles City (Ordinance 424, s. 2017), a.k.a. Kapampángan Language Ordinance.

PÁMAGLÁBUNG
Expanding Domains

Within the last decade, Kulitan has become more visible in several domains. It is no longer surprising to see the indigenous Kapampángan script on product labels and a number of shop signs.

Somewhere in Dau, Mabalacat, one could encounter a Kapampángan directional sign with Kulitan script pointing towards the location of the Next Generation Gym (G2K) [Fig. 67].

Figure 67. The Kapampángan phrase "Keni pû (This way)" is written in Kulitan. The word DÁYÎ 'generation, race' is likewise written on the logo of G2K.

In Barangay Santo Cristo, behind the *Iglesia ni Cristo* church building, there is a traditional Kapampángan eatery called *Taldáwâ: Pipánganan Bíbi at Kambíngan.* Not only do they serve the best *Sigang Kambing* (mutton in sour broth) and *Kaldarétang Bíbi* (duck roasted in tomatoes), you can also read Kulitan on a red seal pattern on their signage within their compound.

In Barangay Cutcut in Angeles City, on the road to Porac, one may encounter a small eatery called *Silió* with its name boldly written in Kulitan. SILIÓ is the Kapampángan word for 'bowl.' There are said to be other establishments with Kulitan script found on their signage in Guagua, Apalit and other parts of Pampanga.

Of course, there is the *Sálángí Kó Pû* Variety Store on Jesus Street in downtown Angeles City that is owned and managed by Kulitan calligrapher and entrepreneur, *Taram Kalis* (Eugene David Ngo). *Taram Kalis* also designs t-shirts, mugs and other gift items printed with his bold Kulitan calligraphy.

In the heartland of the Tagalog imperialist capital is *Pampanga Sísig Spot* in Fairview, Quezon City, which is owned by Kapampángan cultural activist Froilan Pacia Tadeo of San Fernando. Tadeo aims not only to introduce authentic Kapampángan *Sizzling Sísig Bábî*, a dish that has been misappropriated and perverted by the Tagalogs in the capital, but also express the shop's authentic Kapampángan identity through the indigenous Kapampángan script, Kulitan. Not only is the Kapampángan word SÍSIG written in Kulitan on its fiery red signage, the interior design has the iconic Kapampángan song *Atin ku pung Singsing* written in Kulitan as well [Fig. 68].

Kulitan has been well-incorporated in the interior designs of several business establishments. Most remarkable of these is the interior of *Singku Café* that is located within Angeles City's Heritage District [Fig. 69]. It is owned and managed by Kapampángan cultural advocates, Rio Guevarra of Lubao and Jiro Garbes of the Garbes clan of San Fernando. The interior was designed by Kulitan writer and cultural activist, Marlo (Mark Laurenz) Garcia of Mabalacat.

The most ubiquitous display of Kulitan in any business establishment can perhaps be found in the interior of the Newpoint Mall at the Nepo Complex in Angeles City. "*Sálángí kó pû*," the phrase used by upland Kapampángans in welcoming guests, is written in illuminated Kulitan

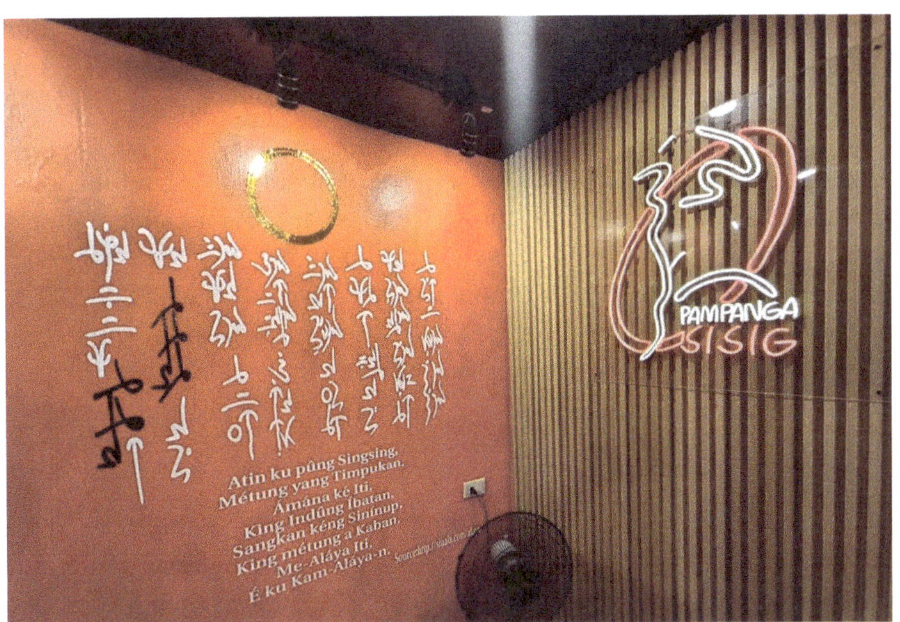

Figure 68. This is the interior design of the Pampanga Sisig Spot (Pasipot) in Fairview, Quezon City.

Figure 69. The interior of Singku Café designed by Marlo Garcia.

and displayed on the four sides of every building post within the mall. The mall is managed by Kapampángan cultural advocate, Trixie Nepomuceno Valdez.

What is unusual is the regular use of Kulitan by a multinational corporation, particularly by the Korean-owned Widus International Leisure, Inc. that operated hotels and casinos at the Clark Freeport Zone. Its CSR (Corporate Social Responsibility) arm, the Widus Foundation, Inc. (WFI), has been has been holistic in their approach in helping the surrounding communities by making sure that the people's pride in their culture is never overlooked even if the project is purely educational or medical.

WFI has been quite prolific promoting Kapampángan cultural heritage, particularly the indigenous script, Kulitan, in their outreach programs within the Kapampángan depressed communities surrounding Clark. This is thanks mainly to WFI's forward thinkers ~ its executive director, Neki Liwanag, and its manager, Ron Golimlim [Fig. 70]

Figure 70. The Kapampángan word SAGIP 'to rescue' is written in Kulitan on the ambulance donated by the Widus Foundation, Inc. (WFI) to the local government (LGU) of Capas in the province of Tarlac. The Widus Foundation calls the ambulance by its Kapampángan name, Saken a Pániagip or literally, "rescue vehicle.

For Kapampángans, the most culturally significant projects of the WFI are the establishment of Sínúpan Singsing: Center for Kapampángan Cultural Heritage at the Angeles City Library in 2019 and the artist hub known as *Santúngan ning Kalalangan* at the loop of the Ábacan Bridge in Angeles City in 2022. The Widus Foundation, Inc. made sure that the indigenous Kapampángan script played a dominant role in establishing the two cultural institutions.

In the recent years, the indigenous Kapampángan script can be seen printed on a number of banners, posters and magazines produced by the Clark chapter of the United Architects of the Philippines (UAP Clark). A Kulitan workshop has also been recently organized for its members. Ironically, this move to promote Kapampángan cultural advocacy was initiated by a non-Kapampángan, Architect Paul Marc Maiquez.

What is most unexpected is to see the indigenous script being used and prominently displayed on important events by a number of private schools such as Don Bosco Academy. Instead of the usual toga, the graduating high school batch of 2021 were made to wear a SALAMPÉ, a graduation sash with the Kapampángan word PÁMAGBÁYU 'change' or 'renewal' written in Kulitan [Fig. 71].

Figure 71. Pablo Augusto M. Hizon of Don Bosco Academy proudly wears his graduation sash with the word PÁMAGBÁYU 'renewal' written in Kulitan. Photo courtesy of Dalsa Hizon.

For the record though, the first academic institution to use the SALAMPÉ as a graduation sash with embroidered Kulitan text was St. Nicholas Academy Center for Catholic Education, Inc. in Macabebe. This is due to the influence of its school principal, Rey Yúmang, a Kapampángan cultural advocate and alumni of the University of the Philippines in Diliman. It was done at a time when it was not yet fashionable to do so.

The SALAMPÉ is an intricately woven piece of cloth worn on the shoulders of Kapampángan males in olden times as a form of social identification. It was recently refashioned by a number of academic institutions in the province of Pampanga as a graduation sash. It was inspired by the "sablay," the graduation sash used by the University of the Philippines. Instead of the Tagalog Baybayin used in the "sablay," the indigenous Kapampángan script, Kulitan, is used in the refashioned SALAMPÉ.

Among public academic institutions, the City College of Angeles (CCA) and the Mabalacat City College (MCC) were among the first to use the refashioned SALAMPÉ as a graduation sash [Fig. 72].

Figure 72. The SALAMPÉ or graduation sash of the City College of Angeles (CCA) with the words Santúngán ning Kabiasnan or 'Sanctuary of Knowledge' embroidered in Kulitan.

Dr. Richard Daenos, president of the City College of Angeles (CCA) from 2017-19, promoted the creation of a curriculum that teaches Kapampángan culture, with the teaching of the indigenous Kapampángan script, Kulitan, as a necessary part of this [Fig. 73]. Kulitan became ubiquitous within the institution. It can be found printed on their diplomas, certificates, trophies, medals, journals, banners, pins, t-shirts, ID lanyards and graduation sashes.

Figure 73. Test papers showing exams in Kulitan at the City College of Angeles (CCA).

Quite unusual is to see the indigenous Kapampángan script at a government event on local television. In December 2019, Kulitan was prominently displayed at the *Mutiá ning Kapampángan*, an annual event held by the provincial government of Pampanga. It is a beauty pageant that was often ridiculed as a poor provincial copy of the *Binibining Pilipinas*, likewise mocked as a third world version of the Miss Universe beauty pageant.

In 2019, the *Mutiá ning Kapampángan* had a thorough cultural makeover, thanks to Randy del Rosario, a Kapampángan cultural advocate belonging to the Kapampángan musical theatre group, *ArtiSta. Rita*, who was made the creative head of the said event. Except for the hosts who have already been hired in advanced, the entire theme was in Kapampángan. This included prayers, songs and gowns. The Kulitan script became the anchor to its Kulitan identity. Not only was the name of the event written in Kulitan, but also the names of every Kapampángan town that participated. Aljon (Albert Jonah) Medina of the Águman Sínúpan Singsing, Inc. was commissioned to do the scripts.

What is probably astonishing is seeing the indigenous Kapampángan script on the logo of the local branch of a national government agency. The Department of Interior and Local Government of Pampanga (DILG Pampanga) have decided in 2022 May 2 to include Kulitan in their own LGRC (Local Governance Resource Center) logo and use it publicly in their posters and infographics [Fig. 74]. Ironically, the Philippine state is seen by many Kulitan writers and activists as the destroyer of Kapampángan language and culture. Its local agencies are seen as nothing more than instruments of Tagalog Imperialism. It is surprising therefore to see the local branch of a national government agency using Kulitan in their logo.

Figure 74. The DILG Pampanga has incorporated Kulitan into their LGRC logo.

PÁMANATÍLÎ

Keeping the Tradition Alive

Now that Kulitan has become more visible in various domains, people wonder if there are still writers who maintain its sanctity with its *Pangílin* "taboos' and *Sangsálâ* 'prohibitions;' if there are those who continue to write Kulitan to write talismans and curses or communicate ancestral spirits.

Fortunately, Kóng Amiél (Amiel Guanlao), a Kapampángan extremist from Wáwâ (Guagua) and Angeles City, maintains this tradition alive. Kóng Amiel is known for his very effective GÚNÂ 'charms' and SUMPÂ 'curses.' They are said to be quite potent because they are written in Kulitan, thereby making them readable by the ancestral gods and the local spirits who would carry out the curse or protection [Fig. 75].

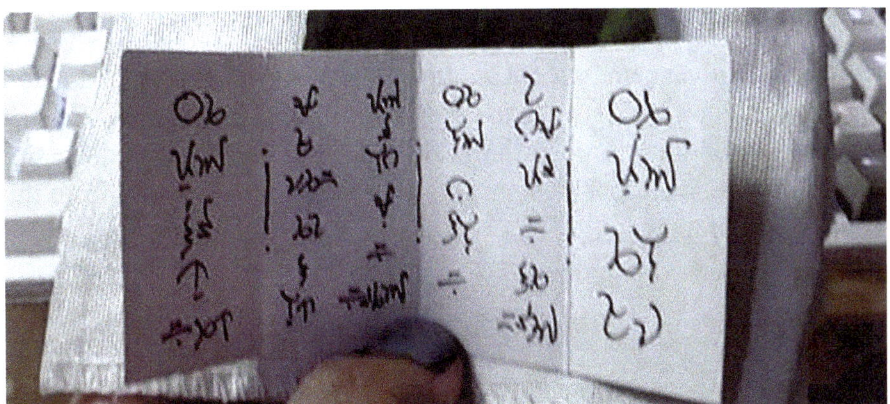

Figure 75. GUNÂ or protective charms made by Amiel Guanlao. This one written in Kulitan and wrapped in a white cloth with Tanglé (Premna odorata) leaves, invoking the protection of Ápung Sínukuan, the Kapampángan sun god.

In 2019 September 6, a final memorial was held for the late Angelo Melo, popularly known as Long, a Kapampángan visual artists and one of the pioneers in indigenous Kapampángan art. The memorial was organized by the Águman Kalalangan Súlat Kapampángan (AGKAS) and the Sunlag Ensemble. Prayers and petitions were written in Kulitan and later burned as part of tradition to appease the spirit of the dearly departed [Fig. 76].

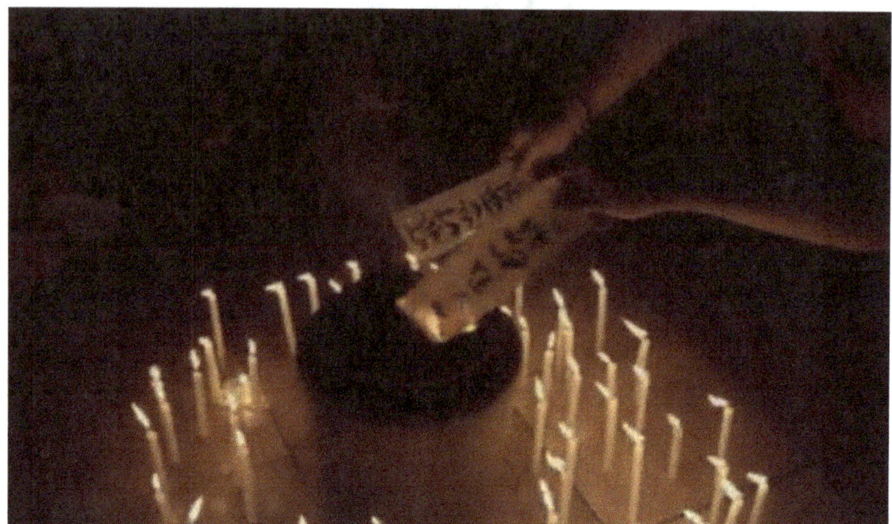

Figure 76. DÁUN kang Long Mélô. Prayers and petitions written in Kulitan were burned to appease the soul of Kapampángan visual artist, Angelo Melo of Angeles City.

Despite the advancement of Kulitan by the youth in social media and digital technology and its use in earthly communications, there are still those who continue to keep the traditions of maintaining the sanctity of the indigenous Kapampángan script alive and passing it down to the younger generation.

SÚSUG I
Appendix I

The following paper was presented at the panel Indic scripts at the 13th International Conference on Austronesian Linguistics (13 ICAL) held at the Academia Sinica, Taipei, Taiwan on 2015 July 18-23, and later posted on: http://ical13.ling.sinica.edu.tw/Full_papers_and_ppts_July_21.htm.

Accurately representing Kapampángan phonology through the KAMBAL SIUÁLÂ 'twin vowels' spelling convention in KULITAN
Siuálâ ding Meángûbié
(Michael Raymon M. Pangilinan)
http://siuala.com
Águman Súlat Kapampángan

Introduction

It has been argued many times that the Romanisation of the Kapampángan language does not accurately represent the sounds of the Kapampángan language. Whether this Romanisation is in SÚLAT BACÚLUD, the Spanish-style orthography introduced by the friars in the 17th century, or in SÚLAT WÁWÂ, the indigenized one introduced by the Philippine revolutionaries in the late 19th century (Pangilinan, 2006b), a number of Kapampángan writers find these inadequate (Pangilinan, 2012a). For instance, Kevin Bätscher, a Ph.D. student at the University of Hawaii who made a preliminary study on the phonology of the Kapampángan language and Súlat Kapampángan (Kulitan), pointed out in a personal communication (2014 December 27) that the Kapampángan sound represented by the Roman letters <Aa> does not sound like Spanish, Japanese or even Tagalog [ɑ] as has been previously thought, but is actually closer to the mid-central vowel [ə] sound similar to the Indonesian letter <e> used in the words "Mag**e**lang" and "M**e**layu," or the open-mid back unrounded vowel [ʌ] in the English word "gun" and "but." Represented by the glyph <⟨glyph⟩> [Fig.1] in Súlat Kapampángan (Kulitan), this [ʌ] or [ə] is clearly different from the [ɑ] found in the Spanish words "casa" or "agua," or the [ɑ] found in the Japanese words は な and かたかな, or even in the Tagalog words "basa" and "bata."

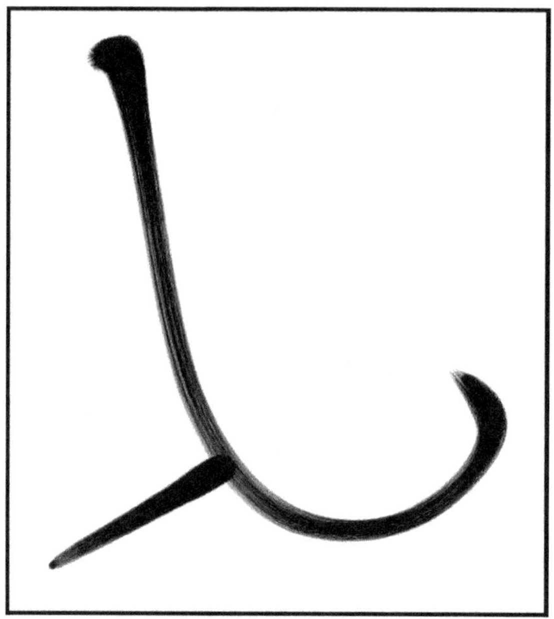

Fig. 1. A [ʌ] or [ə]

It was the Spaniards who first thought of Romanising the Kapampángan language in the 17th century and assigned the Roman letter <Aa> that represented the Spanish vowel sound [ɑ] to the Súlat Kapampángan (Kulitan) vowel glyph on Fig.1 (Benavente, 1699; 2007) [Fig. 2].

Therefore the same goes true for the inherent vowel sound of all the INDÛNG SÚLAT consonant glyphs of Súlat Kapampángan (Kulitan) [Table 1]. Their default vowel sound, though represented by

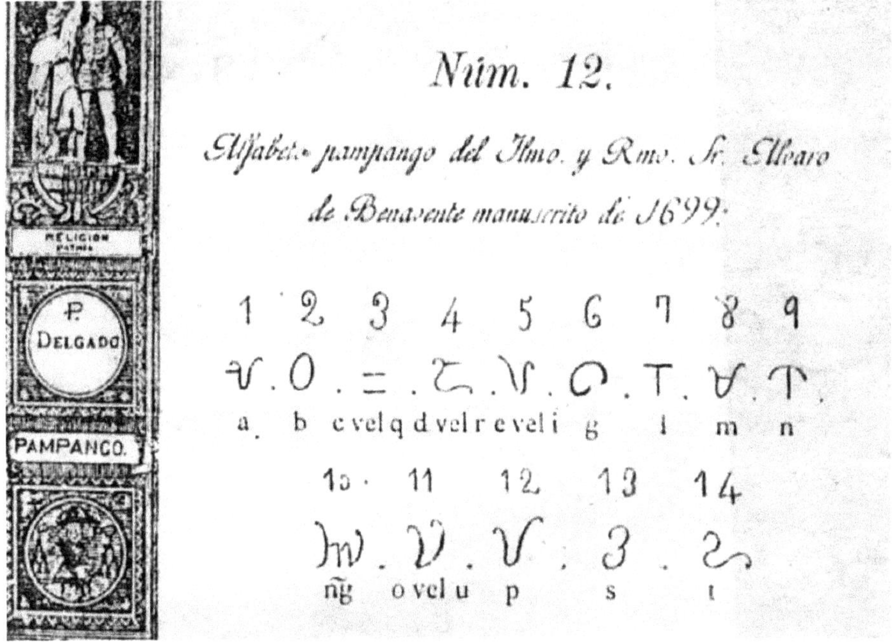

Fig. 2. Súlat Kapampángan (Alfabeto Pampango) recorded by Benavente (1699) as they appear in Marcilla's 1895 Alfabetos Filipinos.

the Roman letter <Aa> in every abecedario and cuaderno (Marcilla, 1895; Hilario, 1962; Henson, 1965 and Pangilinan, 1995 & 2012) does not sound like the [ɑ] vowel sound of Spanish or Tagalog, but something similar to the sounds [ʌ] or [ə] as pointed out by Bätscher.

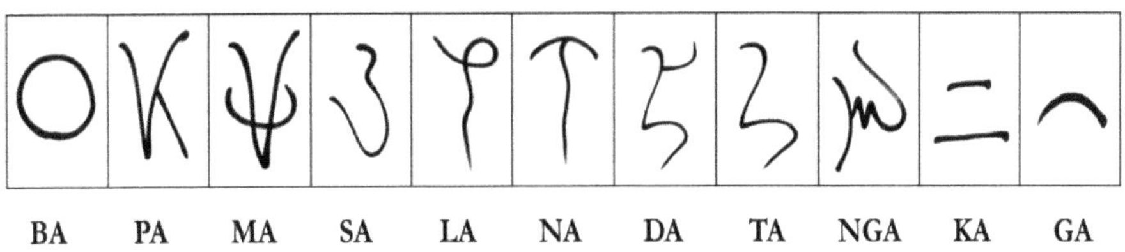

| BA | PA | MA | SA | LA | NA | DA | TA | NGA | KA | GA |

Table 1. The INDÛNG SÚLAT consonantal glyphs in their recital order from right to left.

In Kulitan therefore, the Roman letter <Aa> assigned to a Kapampángan word, for instance MANGAN 'to eat,' the Roman letter <Aa> does not read [ɑ], but rather [ʌ] or [ə]. The word written in Súlat Kapampángan (Kulitan) in [Fig. 3] therefore does not read [maŋan] but rather something like [mʌŋʌn]. Kapampángan still say

229

it as [mʌŋʌn] regardless of how it is written in the Roman script.

Fig. 3. MANGAN 'to eat'

The [ɑ] sound, often Romanized as (á) for medial position and (â) for final position in written Kapampángan is represented by a KAMBAL SIUÁLÂ 'twin vowels' in Súlat Kapampángan (Kulitan) [Table 2 & 3] (Pangilinan, 2012) and attached as a ligature [Fig. 4] to an INDÛNG SÚLAT consonant glyph [Table 1].

Fig. 4. <Áá> (medial) / <Ââ> (final)

For instance, SANG [sʌŋ] in Fig. 5 becomes SÁNG [saŋ] in Fig. 6 by adding the KAMBAL SIUÁLÂ ligature <⟨ ⟩> '-á-/-â' [-ɑ-] in Fig. 4 to INDÛNG SIÚLAT <⟨ ⟩> 'SA' [sʌ] [see Table 1]. Either a new form of Romanisation or orthographic scheme is needed to properly represent these sounds in the Kapampángan language.

Fig. 5. SANG [sʌŋ].

Fig. 6. SÁNG [saŋ].

Due to Romanisation, Kapampángan vowels became limited only to the five vowels that exist in the Spanish language: A, E, I, O, U. Upon careful analysis, the sound of the spoken Kapampángan language seem to more than just five vowels in its repertoire. Table 2 is a chart of the glyphs used in Súlat Kapampángan (Kulitan) that includes vowel sounds that were overlooked by previous Spanish scholars and therefore not included in their *cuadernos* and *abecedarios* (Pangilinan, 2012). These include the KAMBAL SIUÁLÂ 'twin vowels' for the sounds <-á-/-â> [ɑ], <-í-/-î> [i], & <-ú-/-û> [u] that appear as ligatures in [Table 2].

Indûng Súlat	Anak Súlat Vowels						
∧	-ɑ- -ʌ?	I	-i- -ɪ?	ʊ	-u- -ʊ?	ɛ	ɔ

Table 2. A chart representing the diacritical marks and ligatures that alter the default vowel sound of the INDÛNG SÚLAT consonantal glyphs.

231

Linguists who made previous studies into the Kapampángan language have focused mainly on its morphology, syntax and lexicon and only made brief and casual description of its phonology. A detailed study of Kapampángan phonology has not been made so far. This is what is needed to devise a working orthography that could best represent the Kapampángan language in the Roman script. For now, Kapampángans who can still read and write in Súlat Kapampángan (Kulitan) content themselves with the belief and understanding that their indigenous script is the only writing system that properly represents the sounds in their language, most especially with the use of the KAMBAL SIUÁLÂ 'twin vowels' spelling convention.

KAMBAL SIUÁLÂ 'Twin Vowels'

When Súlat Kapampángan (Kulitan) is the only script used to express the Kapampángan language in written form, no two words were spelled exactly the same way. The lengthening of the vowel sounds and final glottal stops, or the stresses and accents in the Kapampángan language, were solely expressed through a spelling convention known as KAMBAL SIUÁLÂ 'twin vowels'.

When the Spanish language, along with the Roman script were taught to the Kapampángan aristocracy who helped administer the colonial government for the Spanish crown, the Kapampángans simply adapted its writing convention in the Romanization of the Kapampángan language. The accents and stresses were clearly indicated by the diacritical marks adopted from written Spanish. The lengthening of the initial and medial vowel sounds were now indicated by the diacritical mark SAKÚRUT <´>, and the final glottal stop by the TELATURUNG <^> diacritical mark (Hilario, 1962 and Pangilinan, 2006a). In Súlat Kapampángan (Kulitan), these sounds are represented distinctly as KAMBAL SIUÁLÂ or 'twin vowels' [See Table 3].

The problem arose when English replaced Spanish as the official language in the early 20th century. This was further compounded by the legal imposition of Tagalog as the Philippine national language around the same era. These languages do not make use of diacritical marks to indicate stress or accents in their written form. After just two gen-

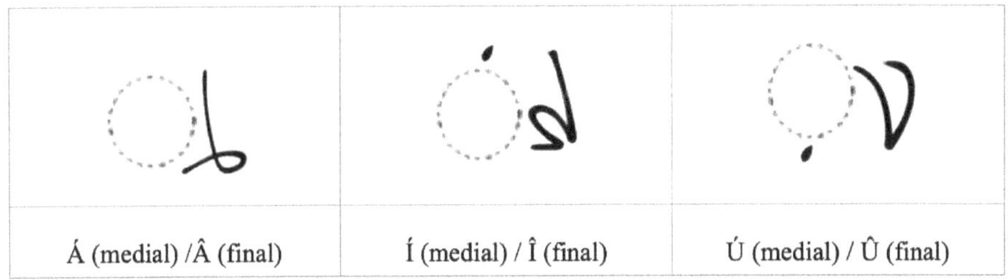

| Á (medial) /Â (final) | Í (medial) / Î (final) | Ú (medial) / Û (final) |

Table 3. The KAMBAL SIUÁLÂ ligatures.

erations of education and exposure to the writing conventions of the English and Tagalog languages, Kapampángan historian Mariano Henson (1965) lamented that the Kapampángan people at the time of his writing can no longer write their language properly in the Roman script. They became ignorant with the proper placement of the diacritical marks. Many simply omitted them. Two or three words spelled the same way but pronounced differently now exist in the Kapampángan written language. As a result, a number of readers often commit the *fallacy of accent*, whereby one confuses two words of the same spelling but with different reading as one and the same word (Bachuber, 1952).

Henson gives the classic example of the words that Kapampángan often mistake in reading and comprehension due to the absence of the necessary diacritical marks: MASAKIT (adj.) 'painful', MASÁKIT (adj.) 'difficult', MÁSAKIT (n.) 'sick person.' In Súlat Kapampángan (Kulitan), these three words would have been written differently [See Table 4].

In Table 4, MASÁKIT (adj.) 'difficult' has an attached KAMBAL SIUÁLÂ ligature < > [-a-] right beside the INDÛNG SIÚLAT glyph < > [sʌ] when written in Súlat Kapampángan (Kulitan). Likewise, MÁSAKIT (n.) 'sick person' has the KAMBAL SIUÁLÂ ligature < > [-a-] right after the ( ) [mʌ]. MASAKIT (adj.) 'painful' does not need a KAMBAL SIUÁLÂ. The difference between the three words is clearly obvious and quite evident when written in Súlat Kapampángan (Kulitan) [See Table 4]. This would show that somehow Súlat Kapampángan (Kulitan) has been specifically designed to represent the phonology of the Kapampángan language in its written form. Ironically, although practically every Kapampángan have been exposed to the Roman script since preschool age, only a very limited few could ac-

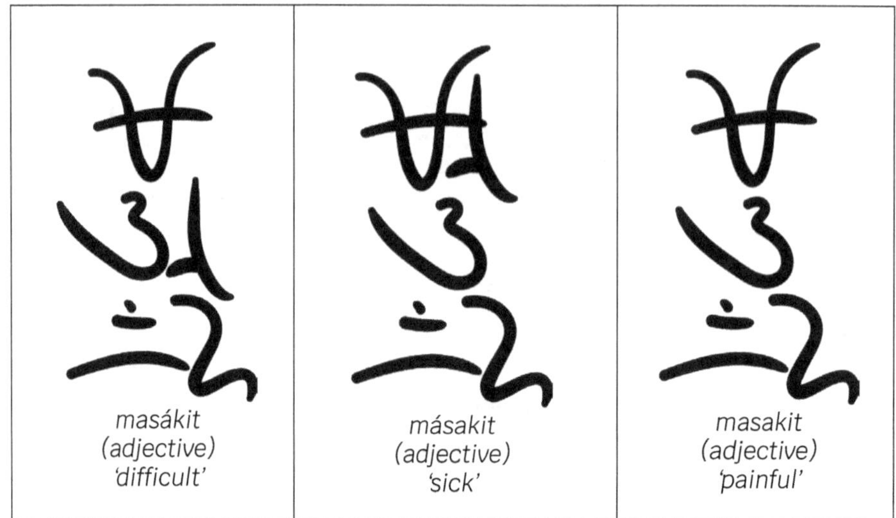

Table 4. The three words above are often misread in Romanized Kapampángan writing, especially when the necessary diacritical marks are misplaced or omitted. In Kulitan, the difference between these words is obviously evident.

curately represent the sound of their language in this very same script. If the necessary diacritical marks have been misplaced or completely omitted when writing Kapampángan in the Roman script, the meaning of each word is compromised. If generations of Kapampángan writers since Henson's time have been ignoring the use of the diacritical marks in written Kapampángan, then the teaching and study of the Kapampángan language through its contemporary literature is also highly compromised. The current generation, especially those who were born abroad or raised speaking Tagalog at home, will find it hard to relearn to speak the language of their parents and grandparents if the existing literature does not accurately represent the phonology of the Kapampángan language.

Súlat Kapampángan (Kulitan)

Súlat Kapampángan (Kulitan), the indigenous Kapampángan script, is an abugida or alphasyllabary made up basically of fourteen base KU-LIT 'glyph' classified as INDÚNG SÚLAT 'mother script'. These INDÚNG SÚLAT glyphs are made up of twelve consonants [see also Table 1] and three basic vowels [see Fig. 7]. Also classified as INDÚNG SÚLAT but are strictly speaking ANAK SÚLAT 'offspring script' are the two monop-

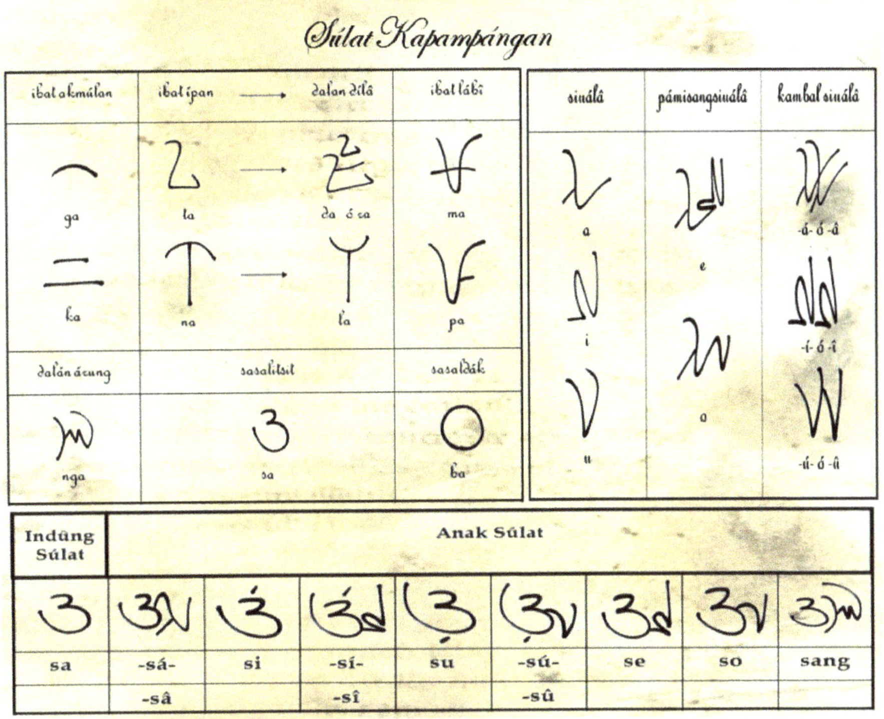

Súlat Kapampángan

Fig. 7. Súlat Kapampángan (Kulitan), the indigenous Kapampángan script.

thongized diphthongs known as PÁMISANGSIUÁLÂ. The diphthongs AI and AU have long been monophthongized in the Kapampángan language (Gonzales, 1972) and represented as E and O respectively in Romanised Kapampángan (Hilario, 1962) [Fig. 7 and see also Table 2].

The three the KAMBAL SIUÁLÂ or 'twin vowels' portrayed in Figure 7 [see also Table 2 & 3] are not a separate set of vowel compounds. They are not classified as ANAK SÚLAT. Rather, they are a PÁMANGANAK SÚLAT 'giving birth to ANAK SÚLAT,' a spelling convention that represents a lengthened medial vowel sound or a final glottal stop. However, they are always listed next to the SIUÁLÂ 'vowels' and the monophthongized diphthongs, PÁMISANGSIUÁLÂ, to remind the person learning Súlat Kapampángan (Kulitan) that KAM-

BAL SIUÁLÂ vowel sounds exist in the Kapampángan language.

INDÛNG SÚLAT and ANAK SÚLAT (Pangilinan, 2012b)

The INDÛNG SÚLAT or 'mother script' are the KULIT or glyphs with their inherent vowel sounds unaltered. They are the building blocks of writing or PÁMANIÚLAT. When their inherent vowel sound is altered with the use of the GARLIT 'diacritical marks', as well as a PÁMISANGSIUÁLÂ or a KAMBAL SIUÁLÂ ligatures, a new glyph is born. This new glyph is called the ANAK SÚLAT 'offspring script.' Any combination of two or more INDÛNG SÚLAT glyph would result in the PÁMANGANAK 'birthing' of an ANAK SÚLAT, hence the term PÁMANGANAK SÚLAT 'giving birth to ANAK SÚLAT'. PÁMANGANAK SÚLAT are the spelling rules and conventions in KULITAN.

INDÛNG SÚLAT Consonantal Glyphs

The INDÛNG SÚLAT consonants are the base characters with the unaltered

1. From the AKMÚLAN (velum), we have GA (⌒) and KA (=);
2. DALÁN KING ÁRUNG (velar nasal) we have NGA (‿);
3. From the ÍPAN (teeth), we have TA (Ɀ) and NA (Ϯ);
4. DALÁN KING DÍLÂ (alveoli), we have DA/RA (ᚹ) and LA (Υ);
5. For the PASALITSIT KING ÍPAN (fricative), we have SA (Ꝡ);
6. From the LÁBÎ (bilabia), we have MA (ᚻ) and PA (ᚺ);
7. For the PATIÚP KING LÁBÎ (aspirated bilabial), we have BA (◯).

inherent vowel sounds. They are arranged according to the where the sound originates. There are 7 sets (Pangilinan, 2012b) [see Table 1 and Fig. 8]:

The recital order is GA, KA, NGA, TA, DA, NA, LA, SA,

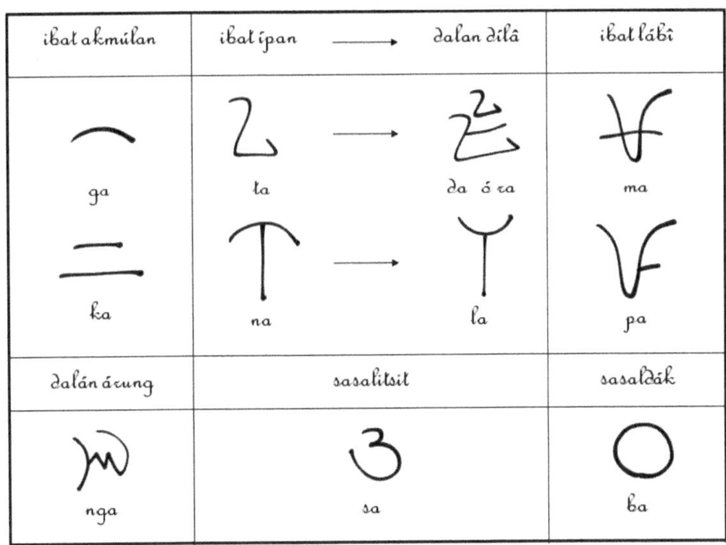

Fig. 8. The twelve INDÛNG SÚLAT consonantal characters.

MA, PA and BA [Table 1]. Take note that the default vowel sound of each INDÛNG SÚLAT consonantal glyph represented by the Roman letter <Aa> sounds like [ʌ] or [ə] rather than [ɑ].

SIUÁLÂ (Vowels)

Strictly speaking, the vowels in Súlat Kapampángan (Kulitan), known as SIUÁLÂ, are the GARLIT 'diacritical marks' placed above or below an IN-

Indûng Súlat	Anak Súlat						
sa	-sá- (medial)	si	-sí- (medial)	su	-sú- (medial)	se	so
	-sâ (final)		-sî (final)		-sû (final)		

Table 5. Altering the inherent vowel sound of the INDÛNG SÚLAT glyph 'SA' by means of the GARLIT, PÁMISANGSIUÁLÂ ligatures and KAMBAL SIUÁLÂ ligatures.

DÛNG SÚLAT consonantal glyph that alters its inherent vowel sound [ʌ] or [ə] (rather than [ɑ]) to something close to [ɪ] when placed above it or to [ʊ] when placed below it. These sounds are however simply represented by the Roman letters <Ii> and <Uu> respectively [See Table 5 and also Table 2]. The PÁMISANGSIUÁLÂ (monophthongized diphthongs) and KAMBAL

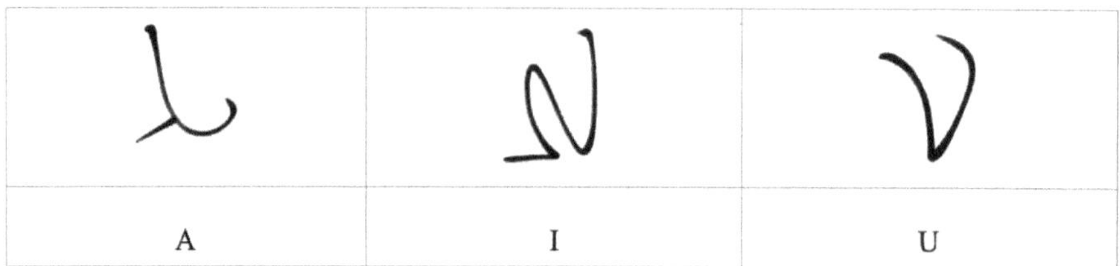

A	I	U

Table 6. The INDÛNG SÚLAT SIUÁLÂ or vowels when written independently or in the initial position. Note that I and U can act as consonants the sound of which can be altered by diacritical marks.

SIUÁLÂ are attached as ligatures that alter the inherent [ʌ] or [ə] of any INDÛNG SÚLAT consonantal glyphs [See Table 2 and 5]. When the vowels are in the initial position or stand alone as INDÛNG SÚLAT, they are basically <ᒪ> [ʌ] or [ə], <ᑍ> [ɪ] and <ᐱ> [ʊ] [see Table 2 and 6].

The PÁMISANGSIUÁLÂ (monophthongized diphthongs)

Strictly speaking, the vowel glyphs (ᒪᶜᵛ) [ɛ], represented by the Roman letter <E>, and (ᒪᵛ) [ɔ], represented by the Roman letter <O>, are ANAK SÚLAT and not INDÛNG SÚLAT, since they are each ADDUÂNG KULIT A MÉGING MÉTUNG MÛ (Hilario, 1962) or 'two KULIT (glyphs) fused into one'. <E> (ᒪᶜᵛ) is a monophthongized form of the diphthong (ᒪᶜᵛ) [ʌɪ] or [əɪ] and therefore the ANAK SÚLAT of the INDÛNG SÚLAT glyph (ᒪ) [ʌ] or [ə] and (ᑍᵛ) [ɪ]. <O> (ᒪᵛ) is likewise the ANAK SÚLAT of

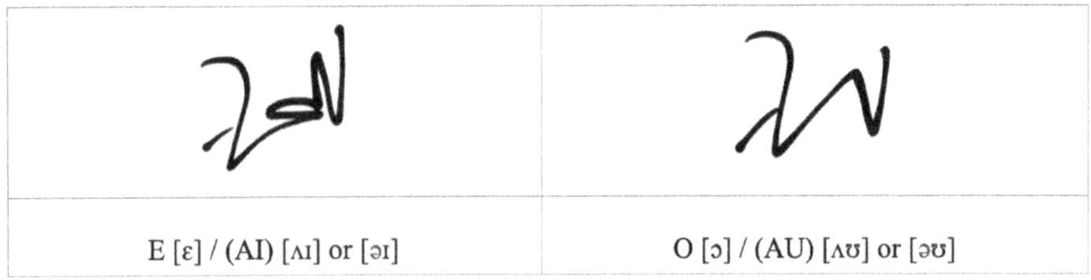

E [ɛ] / (AI) [ʌɪ] or [əɪ]	O [ɔ] / (AU) [ʌʊ] or [əʊ]

Table 7. The PÁMISANGSIUÁLÂ (monophthongised diphthongs) as they appear in their initial form

the INDÛNG SÚLAT glyph (ᒻ)[ʌ] or [ə] and (ᐯ) [ʊ], a monophthongized form of the diphthong (ᒻᐯ) [ʌʊ] or [əʊ]. For generations now, (ᒻᒉ) [ɛ] and (ᒻᐯ) [ɔ] have been treated as INDÛNG SÚLAT even if they strictly speaking ANAK SÚLAT. For the sake of simplicity and in line with their current treatment, we will consider them as INDÛNG SÚLAT in this paper

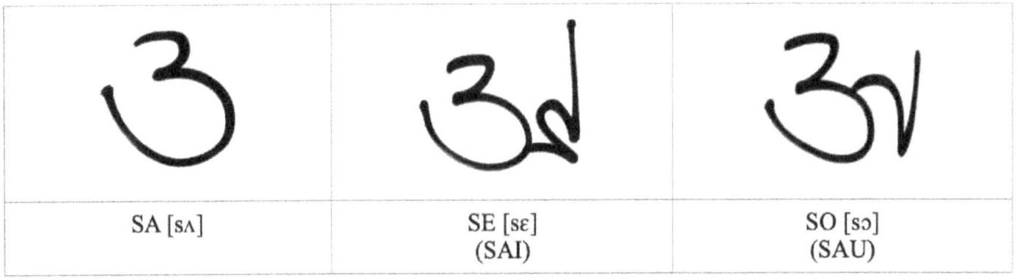

SA [sʌ]	SE [sɛ] (SAI)	SO [sɔ] (SAU)

Table 8. Altering the inherent vowel sound of INDÛNG SÚLAT glyph 'SA' by means of the PÁMISANGSIUÁLÂ ligatures.

and represented simply by the Roman letters <E> and <O> respectively.

These monophthongized diphthongs however commonly appear as ligatures attached to an INDÛNG SÚLAT consonant glyph [See Table 2 & 8]. Since INDÛNG SÚLAT consonants already possess and inherent vowel sound 'A', one merely attached the vowel glyph 'I' (ᒉ) as a ligature to form the vowel sound 'E', and the vowel glyph 'U' (ᐯ) as a ligature to form the vowel sound 'O' [See Table 6].

Normally, KAMBAL SIUÁLÂ appear as extra vowel ligatures attached either to an INDÛNG SÚLAT glyph or a modified ANAK SÚLAT glyph. Examples of INDÛNG SÚLAT glyphs with attached KAMBAL SIUÁLÂ ligatures are those given in Table 3 and 4. In Table 4, the 'MÁ' of the word MÁSAKIT (n.) 'sick person' in contains the KAMBAL SIUÁLÂ ligature <⌣> right after the <Ⱶ> [mʌ] to form the ANAK SÚLAT compound glyph <Ⱶ⌣> [ma], which is written as <MÁ> in the Roman alphabet. The word MASÁKIT (adj.) 'difficult' on the other hand has an attached KAMBAL SIUÁLÂ ligature <⌣> right beside the glyph <ꓱ> [sʌ] to form <ꓱ⌣> [sɑ], written in Roman letters as <SÁ>.

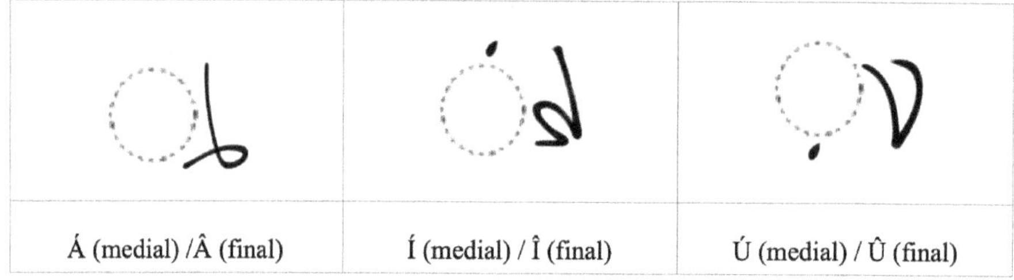

Á (medial) / Â (final)	Í (medial) / Î (final)	Ú (medial) / Û (final)

[Reposting] Table 3. The KAMBAL SIUÁLÂ ligatures.

Examples of ANAK SÚLAT modified by KAMBAL SIUÁLÂ ligatures [Table 3] can be found in Table 5. In that example, the [ɪ] sound of ANAK SÚLAT glyph <ꓱ> [sɪ] is further lengthened to [i] in the medial position or as [ɪʔ] in the final position when the KAMBAL SIUÁLÂ ligature <ꓵ> is placed right next to <ꓱ>. Hence <ꓱ> [sɪ] becomes <ꓱꓵ> [si] or <ꓱꓵ> [sɪʔ] respectively. In the Roman script, the medial <ꓱꓵ> [si] is written as <SÍ>, while the final position <ꓱꓵ> [sɪʔ] is written as <SÎ>.

Take note that both medial <ꓱꓵ> [si] and final <ꓱꓵ> [sɪʔ] are written in the same way. One though not so popular theory is that the KAMBAL SIUÁLÂ were originally just double vowels that were pronounced distinctly with a glottal stop in between, as in the Tagalog words *pook* [po/ok] 'place' and *saad* [sa-ad] 'to state.' Later, the Kapampángan language simply fused the double vowels into a lengthened vowel sound in medial position and a glottal stop in the final position. <ꓱꓵ> was

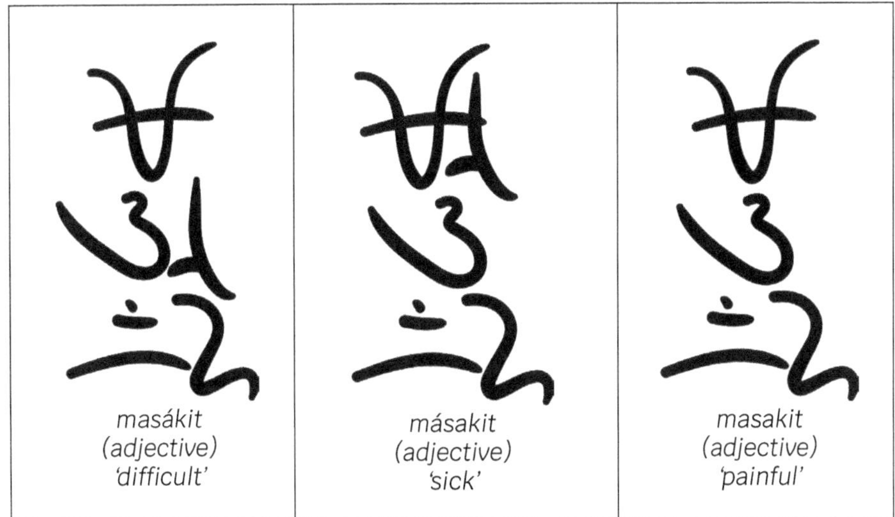

[Reposting] Table 4. The three words above are often misread in Romanized Kapampángan writing, especially when the necessary diacritical marks are misplaced or omitted. In Kulitan, the difference between these words is obviously evident.

therefore said to have been originally articulated as [sɪʔ-ɪʔ] before it evolved into medial [si] and final [sɪʔ]. This however is not an theory among Kapampángan ultranationalist who remain the majority among those who can still read and write Súlat Kapampángan (Kulitan). Interestingly, the final glottal stop in such words becomes lengthened when followed by another word. For instance the [ʊʔ] in the Kapampángan adverb MÛ [mʊʔ] 'only' becomes [u] in MÚ [mu] when the

Indûng Súlat	Anak Súlat							
sa	-sá- (medial)	si	-sí- (medial)	su	-sú- (medial)	se	so
	-sâ (final)		-sî (final)		-sû (final)		

[Reposting] Table 5. Altering the inherent vowel sound of INDÛNG SÚLAT glyph 'SA' by means of the GARLIT, PÁMISANGSIUÁLÂ ligatures and KAMBAL SIUÁLÂ ligatures.

Fig. 9. MÛ (adv. <mʊʔ>) 'only'

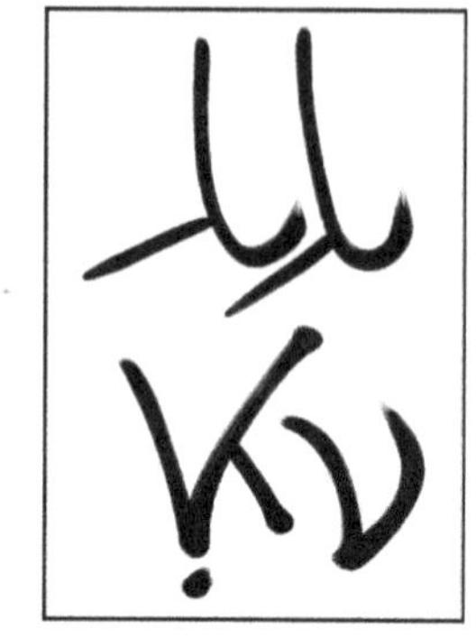

Fig. 10. ÁPÛ [ɑpuʔ] 'grandmother'

adverb RIN 'also' follows it. These can be demonstrated in the following phrases: *yáku mû* [mʊʔ] 'only me' and *iká mú* [mu] *rin* 'only you also.' In Súlat Kapampángan (Kulitan) however, these two distinct sounds are simply written in the same way: <𝕐𝓋> [Fig. 9]. KAMBAL SIUÁLÂ are not only attached as vowel ligatures in Súlat Kapampángan (Kulitan). They can also be written in the initial position like the <Á> [ɑ] in the word ÁPÛ [ɑpuʔ] 'grandmother' [Fig. 10]. Table 9 shows the KAMBAL SIUÁLÂ as they appear in initial position and not as vowel ligatures. Compare these to Table 3.

Á (medial) / Â (final)	Í (medial) / Î (final)	Ú (medial) / Û (final)

Table 9. The KAMBAL SIUÁLÂ when they are written in the initial position and not as ligatures. Compare these to Table 3.

Fallacy of Accent

Strictly speaking, words having different accents are not the same word (Bachuber, 1952). A fallacy of accent occurs when two words of the same spelling but with different reading are confused as one and the same word. The Kapampángan language contains many words that are spelled the same way but pronounced differently when written in the Roman script. With the absence of the necessary diacritical marks in the current Romanized form of the Kapampángan language, the meaning of such words are often compromised, especially when one cannot totally rely on the context of how they were used (Pangilinan, 2006a). In a folktale written by Ernesto Turla (1999) in his self-published Kapampángan dictionary, one cannot determine the meaning of the word SUSU in the title DENG SUSU NANG LUNINGNING because of the absence of diacritical marks or any form of pronunciation guide. In the Kapampángan language, SÚSU [susʊ] could either mean 'breast' or SUSÛ [sʊsuʔ] 'snail'. Upon reading the folktale, one will still not be able to determine from the context whether the SUSU in the story referred to the goddess Lun-

Fig. 11. Súlat Kapampángan (Kulitan) writer Jayvie Suasi Aboyme makes a parody of the word SUSU that appears in the narrative Ding Susu Nang Luningning by Ernesto Turla (1999). Is it SÚSU [susʊ] 'breast' or SUSÛ [sʊsuʔ] 'snail?'

ingning's breast or pet snails as the story takes place at a waterfall. Is it her breasts that were wet and slippery because of the mists from the sacred waterfall? Or did she have a pair of pet snails that are beautiful to look at but are very disobedient and liked to move on their own? In Súlat Kapampángan (Kulitan), the distinction between SÚSU [susʊ] 'breast' or SUSÛ [sʊsuʔ] 'snail' is easily distinguished at a glance with the use of the KAMBAL SIUÁLÂ (Fig. 12). No two words are written in the same way in Súlat Kapampángan (Kulitan). Therefore, the Fallacy of Accent can not occur. Unfortunately, this is not the case in Romanised Kapampángan, especially when the necessary diacritical marks or any form of pronunciation guides have been neglected or omitted.

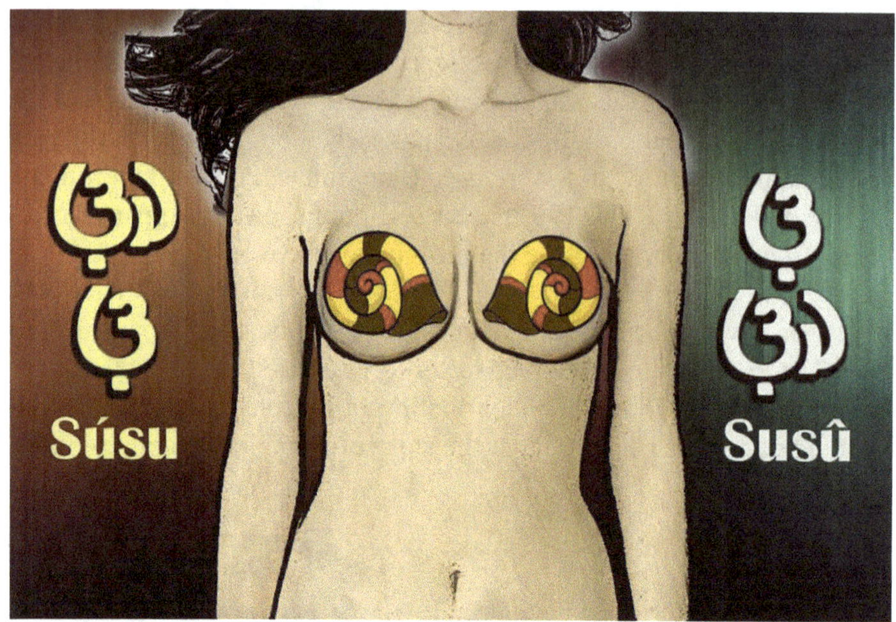

Fig. 12. US-based Kulitan writer Avery Canda Supan demonstrates that in Súlat Kapampángan (Kulitan), the difference between SÚSU [susʊ] 'breast' or SUSÛ [sʊsuʔ] 'snail' is evidently clear at a glance.

Here are a few Kapampángan words taken from Pangilinan's 10 ICAL Paper (2006), where one can easily commit the Fallacy of Accent if the necessary diacritical marks or any form of pronunciation guide are not in place. These words are never written in the same way when written in Súlat Kapampángan (Kulitan) because of the KAMBAL SIUÁLÂ spelling convention.

SÚSU (n.) 'breast'	SUSÛ (n.) 'snail'
SÍSI (v.) 'to regret'	SÍSÎ (n.) 'chick'
KÚKÛ (n.) 'cough'	KUKÛ (n.) 'finger nail'
BÁBÂ (n.) 'chin'	BABÂ (n.) 'to put down'
SALÁT (v.) 'to touch (sexually)'	SÁLAT (n.) 'blemish'
ANAK (n.) 'child'	ÁNAK (n.) 'children'
BABÁYI (n.) 'woman'	BÁBÁYI (n.) 'women'
LALÁKI (n.) 'man'	LÁLÁKI (n.) 'men'

Table 10. Kapampángan words spelled the same way when written in the Roman script but pronounced differently and therefore have different meanings (Pangilinan, 2006b).

Since the few who can write Kapampángan in the Roman script are now ignorant with the proper placement of the necessary diacritical marks, one can never avoid creating a scandal whenever reading something in public. For instance, a local news anchor who was reading the weather in Kapampángan on public television in 2008 often created a scandal when he read what should have been the Northeast monsoon into something quite indecent. The Northeast monsoon in Kapampángan is SALÁTAN [sʌlatʌn] and not SÁLATAN [salʌtʌn] 'an orgy of sexual fondling'.

Fig. 13. SALÁTAN [sʌlatʌn]
'Northeast Monsoon'

Fig. 14. SÁLATAN [salʌtʌn]
'a sexual fondling orgy'

If these were written in KULITAN, the scandal could have been avoided since the difference between SALÁTAN [sʌlatʌn] 'Northeast Monsoon' and SÁLATAN [salʌtʌn] 'an orgy of sexual fondling' would have been obvious through the KAMBAL SIUÁLÂ spelling convention. The KAMBAL SIUÁLÂ ligature <  > is clearly visible in the second syllable of SALÁTAN [sʌlatʌn] 'Northeast Monsoon' [Fig. 13] and in the first syllable of SÁLATAN [sɑlʌtʌn] 'an orgy of sexual fondling' [Fig. 14].

Due to current state of Romanization in Kapampángan writing, committing the Fallacy of Accent has become quite common due to the omission of diacritical marks or any form of pronunciation guide. The Kapampángan language has a large number of words that are spelled the same way but read differently (Pangilinan, 2006a). When Spanish was still the official language of the Philippine Islands, their spelling convention was adopted into Romanised Kapampángan writing. The Spanish orthographic convention made use of diacritical marks to help pronounce Kapampángan words. All that changed when English, and later Filipino (Tagalog), replaced Spanish as the official language of the islands. Diacritical marks are unnecessary and can be omitted in written English and Filipino (Tagalog). Unfortunately, the case is not so in Romanized Kapampángan writing.

Conclusions

Further studies into Kapampángan phonology are very much needed. This will aid in devising an accurate orthography in the Roman script. At the moment, the current orthography used in Romanised Kapampángan is quite limited in accurately representing the sounds of the Kapampángan language. Errors occur commonly when reading and writing Kapampángan in the Roman script due to the absence of the necessary pronunciation guides like the diacritical marks. The context and logic of the written word is often compromised as a result.

In the meantime, it would seem that Súlat Kapampángan (Kulitan) has been perfectly designed to phonologically express the Kapampángan language in written form, as especially demonstrated through the function of the KAMBAL SIUÁLÂ. No two words are written alike. The Fallacy of Accent can hardly occur when the Kapampángan language is written in its indigenous script.

Reviving and popularizing the use of Súlat Kapampángan (Kulitan) in Kapampángan writing today may aid in Kapampángan literacy and the proper study of the language. Knowledge in Súlat Kapampángan (Kulitan) appears to be a necessity in studying Kapampángan phonology.

However, there are certain limits in using Súlat Kapampángan (Kulitan). Given its vertical writing system and its convention of dividing each segment into syllable blocks, they remain quite a challenge for digital encoding (Miller, 2011 and Norman delos Santos, personal communication, 2014 February 28). Literature in Súlat Kapampángan (Kulitan) remains handwritten and therefore difficult to reproduce. Majority of the Kapampángan people look at Súlat Kapampángan (Kulitan) as a mere novelty. They enjoy seeing it in tattoos, in rituals, in signatures, in logos and in art. They swell with pride whenever they see someone who can still read and write in it. However, this same majority sees the need to study and revive the use of Súlat Kapampángan (Kulitan) in everyday communication as impractical and a waste of time in this digital era.

References:

Bachuber, Andrew H. (1952). *Introduction to Logic*. St. Louis, Missouri, USA: Missouri Province Educational Institute, St. Louis University.

Benavente, Alvaro de. (1699). *Arte de Lengua Pampanga*. [Bilingual ed. 2007: Spanish and English]. Transl. Edliberto V. Santos. Angeles City, Philippines: Juan D. Nepomuceno Center for Kapampángan Studies, Holy Angel University.

Gonzales, Andrew. (1972). *Pampangan: Outline of a Generative Semantic Description*. Manila: De La Salle University Press.

Henson, Mariano A. (1965). *The Province of Pampanga and Its Towns: A.D. 1300-1965*. [4th ed. revised]. Angeles City, Philippines: By the author.

Hilario, Zoilo. (1962) *Bayung Sunis*. [Typescript].

Marcilla, Cipriano M. (1895). *Estudio de los Antiguos Alfabetos Filipinos*. Malabon: Tipo-Litografia del Asilo de Huérfanos.

Miller, Christopher Ray. (2011 March 11). *Indonesian and Philippine*

Scripts and extensions not yet encoded or proposed for encoding in Unicode as of version 6.0: A report for the Berkley Script Encoding Initiative. Retrieved March 23, 2012 from http://www.unicode.org/notes/tn35/indonesian-philippine.pdf.

Pangilinan, Michael R. M. [as Siuálâ ding Meángûbié]. (1995). *Pamagkulit King Kekatamung Matuang Kasulatan.* In Ing Susi, 6:1:24-25.

Pangilinan, Michael R.M. (2006a). *The Importance of Diacritical Marks in Romanized Kapampángan.* 10th International Conference on Austronesian Linguistics (10 ICAL), Puerto Princesa, Palawan, Philippines.

Pangilinan, Michael R.M. (2006b) *Kapampángan or Capampáñgan: Settling the Dispute on the Kapampángan Romanized Orthography.* 10th International Conference on Austronesian Linguistics (10 ICAL), Puerto Princesa, Palawan, Philippines

Pangilinan, Michael R.M. (2012a). *Kulitan, the indigenous Kapampángan script: A possible answer to the unsettled dispute on the Romanized Kapampángan orthography.* NWAV Asia Pacific 2, Tokyo, Japan.

Pangilinan, Michael R. M. [Siuala ding Meangubie]. (2012b). *An introduction to Kulitan, the indigenous Kapampángan script.* Angeles City: Center for Kapampángan Studies.

Turla, Ernesto C. (1999). *Classic Kapampángan Dictionary.* Offprint Copy.

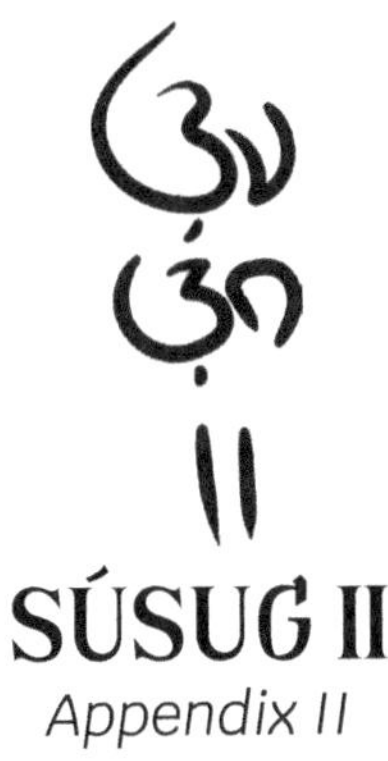

SÚSUG II
Appendix II

An Accurate Kapampángan Orthography

A new orthography to be used in writing KAPAMPÁNGAN in the Roman script was designed by the Ágúman Sínúpan Singsing, Inc. (ASSI), originally for the implementation of Ángeles City's Local Language Code (Ordinance No. 424, Series of 2017) that designated Kapampángan as an official language and institutionalized its use in all sectors.

This KAPAMPÁNGAN orthography was designed in coordination with linguists, language experts and writers of the indigenous script Kulitan. These include Dr. Ricardo Ma. Nolasco and his students from the Department of Linguistics Graduate Studies at the University of the Philippines in Diliman, linguist Kevin Bätscher from the University of Hawaii, and Kapampángan language and script expert, Mike Pangilinan. These scholars have paid keen attention to the phonology of the Kapampángan language and have remained faithful to the indigenous Kapampángan script, **Kulitan**.

Phonology-based Orthography

A. The recital order of Kapampángan consonants, *Ding Sisiwálâ*, originally used in Kulitan, was designed by our ancestors based on the natural articulation of the words in Kapampángan: *ding sisiwálá manibat king akmúlan* 'those pronounced from the throat,' *dalan king*

251

árung 'to the nose', *ibat king ípan* 'from the teeth,' *sasalitsit manibat king ípan* 'hissed from the teeth,' *manibat king lábî* 'from the lips' and *sasaldak manibat king lábî* 'aspirated from the lips.'

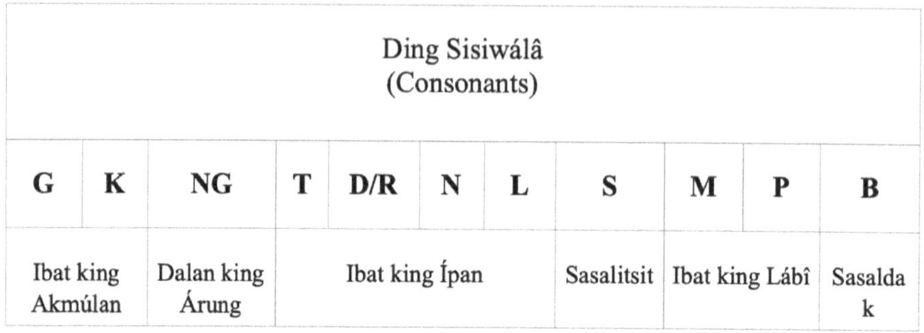

Ding Sisiwálâ (Consonants)										
G	**K**	**NG**	**T**	**D/R**	**N**	**L**	**S**	**M**	**P**	**B**
Ibat king Akmúlan	Dalan king Árung		Ibat king Ípan				Sasalitsit	Ibat king Lábî		Sasaldak

Table 1. Kapampángan consonants based on the indigenous script, Kulitan.

B. The vowels are called *Siwálâ* or 'voice' in the Kapampángan language. The Kapampángan language makes a phonemic distinction between long and short vowels. The default sounds of **A**, **I** and **U** in Kapampángan are shorter and very different from Filipino (Tagalog). For instance the default sound of the letter **A** in Kapampángan is closer to the **O** in the English word "done" than the **A** for "cat." The **A** sound of the Kapampángan word *mangan* 'to eat' is not the same as the **A** sound of the Tagalog word *bahay* 'house' or the Spanish word *casa* 'house.' The default vowel sounds in Spanish and Filipino (Tagalog) are considered long vowels in Kapampángan. Unfortunately these are the sounds that have been taught to them in Philippine schools. The Kapampángan people were conditioned that these too are the default sounds in their language even if by articulation you can prove that they are not. A study of the phonology of the Kapampángan language is therefore very important.

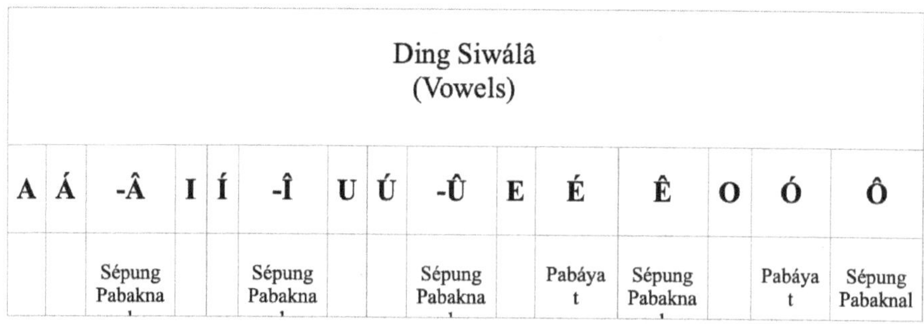

Ding Siwálâ (Vowels)														
A	**Á**	**-Â**	**I**	**Í**	**-Î**	**U**	**Ú**	**-Û**	**E**	**É**	**Ê**	**O**	**Ó**	**Ô**
		Sépung Pabakna			Sépung Pabakna			Sépung Pabakna		Pabáyat	Sépung Pabakna		Pabáyat	Sépung Pabaknal

Table 2. Kapampángan vowels based on phonological studies and the indigenous script, Kulitan.

C.   The long vowels are indicated by the diacritical mark *Sakúrut* [́]. This helps distinguish between, for instance, the words *masakit* 'painful', *masákit* 'difficult' and *másakit* 'sick' by indicating the long vowels. Without this, all of the three words would have been written in the same way and create a fallacy, a misunderstanding and confusion.

D.   The vowels **E** and **O** in Kapampángan used to be the diphthongs **AI** and **AU** respectively *balé* 'house' used to be pronounced as *balai* and *sabó* 'soup' used to be pronounced as sabau. They have become monophthongised about two hundred years ago or so and are therefore pronounce longer than **A**, **I** or **U**. The length of a marked **E** and **O**, i.e. **É** and **Ó** like in *téte* 'bridge' and *sése*, are therefore pronounced longer than usual.

E.   The vowels with the diacritical mark *Télaturung* [^] –**Â**, -**Î**, and –**Û** indicate a *Sépung Pabaknal* or a 'final glottal stop.' The *Télaturung* [^] indicating a final glottal stop distinguishes *sísi* 'to regret' from *sisî* 'chick' and *súsu* 'breast' from *susû* 'snail.'

F.   A final glottal stop marked by a *Télaturung* [^] becomes a long vowel marked by a *Sakúrut* [́] when it loses its final position. For instance, the final vowel -**Î** in "bábî," a final glottal stop marked by a *Télaturung* [^] in the phrase "bulúgan yang bábî," becomes **Í** marked by a *Sakúrut* [́] in "bábí" of the phrase "bábí yang bulúgan" because it is no longer in the final position and has therefore become a long vowel.

G.   The final glottal stops marked by a *Télaturung* [^] are negated when the [–ng] linker is added and become unmarked. For instance, the final vowel -**Û** in "indû" becomes an unmarked **U** in "Indung Kapampángan." The [–ng] linking "indû" with "Kapampángan" removed the sound of the final glottal stop.

H.   In Kapampángan, a final vowel shift often occurs when a declarative sentence becomes an exclamation or an interrogative sentence. The vowels **I** and **U** respectively become the long vowels **É** and **Ó** marked by a *Sakúrut* [́]. For instance, the unmarked final **I** of "bíbi" in the declarative sentence "Mámangan yang bíbi" becomes a final long **É** marked by a *Sakúrut* [́] when the sentence becomes the interrogative "Mámangan yang bíbé?" The final glottal stops in –**Î** and –**Û** marked by a *Télaturung* [^] likewise respectively become marked –**Ê** and –**Ô**. For example, the final glottal stop –**Î** of "násî" in the sentence "Méduluk ing násî" becomes the final glottal stop –**Ê** in the interrogative sentence "Méduluk ing násê?" while the final glottal stop –**Û** of "búkû" in the sentence "Mámangan kang búkû" becomes the final glottal stop –**Ô** in the interrogative sentence "Mámangan kang búkô?"

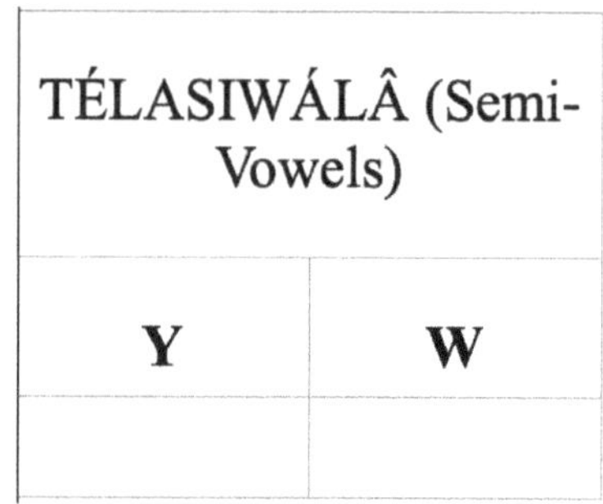

TÉLASIWÁLÂ (Semi-Vowels)	
Y	**W**

Table 3. The semivowels based on the indigenous script, Kulitan.

Although considered outright consonants in many languages, **Y** and **W** are considered *Telasiwálâ* or 'vowel-like' in Kapampángan because they are simply the *Anak Súlat* or derivations of the vowels **I** and **U** in the indigenous Kapampángan script, Kulitan.

Protection Of Heritage Script in accordance with Angeles City's Local Language Code (Ordinance No. 424, Series of 2017):

Section 11. Acknowledgment and Protection of Súlat Kapampángan (Kulitan). The Angeles City Government shall recognize and protect *Súlat Kapampángan*, more popularly known as *Kulitan*, the indigenous and highly endangered Kapampángan script, as a heritage script and institute measures to protect, preserve and promote its use, especially among the youth.

INDUNG SÚLAT: DING SISIWÁLÂ										
(Basic Characters: Consonants)										
Ibat king Akmúlan	Dalan king Árung	Ibat king Ípan					Sasalitsit	Ibat king Lábî		Sasaldak
GA	KA	NGA	TA	DA	NA	LA	SA	MA	PA	BA

Table 4. The basic consonants of the indigenous script, Kulitan.

DING SIWÁLÂ							
(Basic Characters: Initial Vowels)							
A	Á; -Â	I	Í; -Î	U	Ú; -Û	E	O
[ɑ]	[a]; [ɑʔ]	[ɪ]	[i]; [ɪʔ]	[ʊ]	[u]; [ʊʔ]	[ɛ]	[ɔ]

Table 5. The initial vowels.

Indung Súlat	Anak Súlat							
LA	LÁ	LI	LÍ	LU	LÚ	LE	LO	LANG
	-LÂ		-LÎ		-LÛ			

Table 6. Deriving the Anak Súlat, or Kulitan characters with altered vowel sounds, from the Indung Súlat or basic Kulitan characters with their default unaltered vowel sound.

255

SÚSUG III
Appendix III

The names of the Kapampángan speaking municipalities and barangays in Indung Kapampángan

Apálit	Aráyat	Balíuag (Santo Tomas)	Bakúlud (Bacolor)	Bétis	Kandáuâ (Candaba)
Kabagsak (San Luis)	Kuliat (Angeles)	Lubáu (Lubao)	Mabalákat (Mabalacat)	Magálang	Makabébé (Macabebe)
Masantul (Masantol)	Masiku (Mexico)	Minálin	Pinpin (Santa Ana)	Púrak (Porac)	Sampagíta (Floridablanca)
Sampernándu (San Fernando)	San Simun (San Simon)	Santa Ríta	Sasmuán	Wáwâ (Guagua)	Tarlak (Tarlac)
Bangbang (Bamban)	Kápâs (Capas)	Konsepsiun (Concepcion)	Mayúmu (San Miguel, Bulacan)	Mabátang (Abucay, Bataan)	Kalagiman (Samal, Bataan)

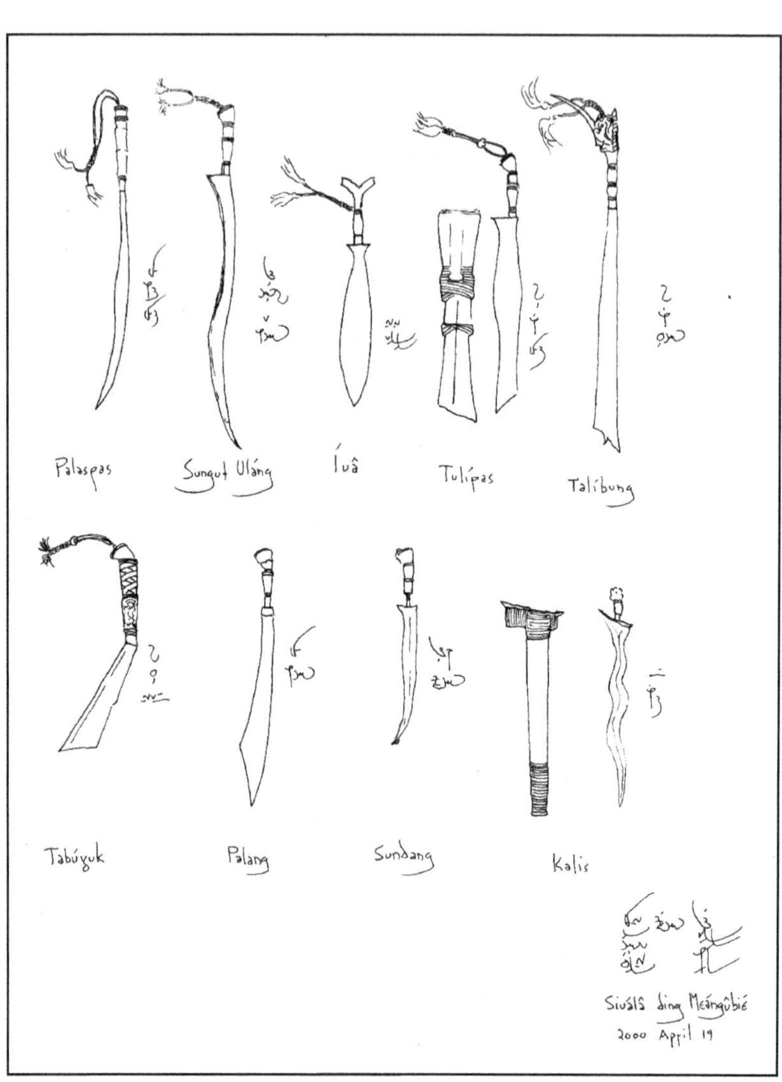

Palaspas
Sungut Uláng
Iuâ
Tulipas
Talibung
Tabúyuk
Palang
Sundang
Kalis
Siuáls ding Meángûbié
2000 April 19

PIKUTNÁNGAN
References

Adi Putra, Rafique. (2010). The Calligraphy of Haji Abdul Hakim Liu Jingyi. In Chinese Muslim Khat. Retrieved 2012 March 16 from http://www.chinesemuslimkhat.com/search/label/gallery.

Alunan, Merlie. (2006 September 19). Writing the National Literature (Why Warays Must Continue Writing in Waray). In merliealunan.blogspot.com. Retrieved March 24, 2012 from http://merliealunan.blogspot.com/2006/09/writing-national-literature-why-warays.html. [Also in DILA, 2007].

Arayata Roslyn. (2009). Laguna Copperplate Inscription: A National Treasure (Photograph). In Roslyn Arayata's Site. Retrieved March 28, 2012 from http://zestybliss.wordpress.com/category/published-work-photograph/.

Ardinez, Akopito. (2010). Sulat Kapampangan. In Akopito. Retrieved March 31, 2012 from http://akopito.weebly.com/suacutelat-kapampaacutengan.html.

Avila, Bobit. (2007 August 24). Ethnic cleansing our own Filipino brethren? In The Philippine Star. Retrieved 2012 March 16 from http://www.philstar.com/Article.aspx?articleId=15037.

Bachuber, Andrew. H. (1952). Introduction to Logic. St. Louis, Missouri: Missouri Province Educational Institute, St. Louis University.

Barari, Jubei. [ばらり重兵衛]. (2007 April 14). Luzon Sukezaemon (呂宋助左衛門). In Barari Jubei no Rekishi Tanbou (ばらり重兵衛の歴史探訪). Retrieved November 17, 2007 from http://www.geocities.jp/bane2161/rusonsukezaemon.html.

Benavente, Alvaro de. (1699). Arte de Lengua Pampanga. [Bilingual ed. 2007: Spanish and English]. Transl. Edliberto V. Santos. Angeles City, Philippines: Juan D. Nepomuceno Center for Kapampangan Studies & The Spanish Program for Cultural Cooperation.

Bergaño, Diego. (1732). Vocabulario de Pampango en Romance y Diccionario de Romance en Pampango. [Bilingual ed. 2006: Spanish and English]. Transl. Venancio Q. Samson. Angeles City, Philippines: Juan D. Nepomuceno Center for Kapampangan Studies & National Commission for Culture and the Arts.

Bergaño, Diego. (1860). Vocabulario de la Lengua Pampanga en Romance. Manila: Imprenta de Ramirez y Giraudier.

Beyer, Henry Otley. (1918). Ethnography of the Pampangan People: A Comprehensive Collection of Original Sources. Vol. 1& 2. Manila, Philippines. [Microfilm].

Beyer, Henry Otley. (1943). A Brief History of Fort Santiago. Manila (no publisher).

Beyer, Henry Otley. (1947 July-August). Outline Review of Philippine Archaeology by Islands and Provinces. In Philippine Journal of Science, LXXVII: 3-4, 226-229.

Berzin, Alexander. (2003). The Life of Atisha. In The Berzin Archives:The Buddhist Archives of Dr. Alexander Berzin. Retrieved June 16, 2009 from http://www.berzinarchives.com.

Blair, Emma H. and Robertson, James A (B&R). (1903-1909). The Philippine Islands 1493-1898. 55 vols. Cleveland: Arthur H. Clark.

Cabuay, Christian. (2012 March 16). Baybayin Bill ~ The National Script Act of 2011. In Baybayin.Com. Retrieved March 23, 2012 from http://www.baybayin.com/baybayin-bill-national-script-act-of-2011/.

Castro, Rosalina Icban. 1981. Literature of the Pampangos. Manila: University of the East Press.

Cavada, Agustin de la. (1876). Historia geográfica, geológica y estadistica de Filipinas. 2 vols. Manila: Ramirez y Giraudier.

Coedès, G. (1918). Le royaumme de Çrīvijaya. In Bulletin de l'Ecole Française d'Extrême-Orient (BEFEO), 18:6:1-36.

Colín, Francisco. (1663). Labor evangélica ministerios apostólicos de los obreros de Compañía de Jesus, fundación y progresos de las Islas Filipinas. Madrid. [1904 ed.] Pablo Pastels. 3 vols. Barcelona. [English translations in] Blair, Emma H. and Robertson, James A. (1903-1909). The Philippine Islands 1493-1898. 55 vols. Cleveland: Arthur H. Clark.

Comandante, Bonifacio F. Jr. (2010). Ancient Baybayin: Early Mother Tongue-based Education Model. In History Ko: Rediscover Filipino Excellence Through History. Retrieved March 28, 2012 from http://www.historyko.org/?q=node/33.

Comandante, Bonifacio F. Jr. (2011). Baybayin Dance: Script Forms Through Time. A paper presented to the 1st Philippine Conference on the Ticao Stones on August 5-6, 2011 at Monreal, Masbate, Philippines. Retrieved March 26, 2008 from http://www2.baybayin360.org/sites/default/files/BAYBAYIN_DANCE_paper.pdf.

Constitution of the Republic of the Philippines. (1899). In Chan Robles Virtual Law Library. Retrieved June 6, 2009 from http://www.chanrobles.com/1899constitutionofthephilippines.htm.

Constitution of the Republic of the Philippines (1987). In Chan Robles Virtual Law Library. Retrieved June 6, 2009 from http://www.chanrobles.com/article14language.htm.

Corpuz, Onofre D. (1989). The Roots of the Filipino Nation. Quezon City, Philippines: AKLAHI Foundation, Inc.

Crawfurd, John. (1856). Descriptive Dictionary of the Indian Islands and Adjacent Countries. London: Bradbury & Evans. PDF format retrieved March 28, 2012 from http://books.google.com.ph/books?id=-5RJAAAAMAAJ&printsec=frontcover&source=gbs_ge_summary_r&cad=0#v=onepage&q&f=false.

Daniels, Peter T. & Bright, William. (1996). The World's Writing Systems, Oxford, U.K.: Oxford University Press.

Defenders of the Indigenous Languages of the Archipelago (DILA). (2007). Filipino is not our language. Angeles City, Pampanga: Defenders of the Indigenous Languages of the Archipelago (DILA).

Del Corro, Anicia H. (1988). A sequel to the dialect study of Kapampangan (1984): With focus on Calaguiman and Mabatang Kapampangan. Diliman, Quezon City, Philippines: University of the Philippines.

Del Corro, Anicia. (2000). Language Endangerment and Bible Translation. Malaga, Spain: Universal Bible Society Triennial Translation Workshop.

Del Corro, Anicia. (2008 December 6). Kapampangan, from the perspective of linguistics. A lecture delivered at the Center for Kapampangan Studies at Holy Angel University in Angeles City.

Diaz, Casimiro. (1745). Conquistas de las Islas Filipinas…Parte Segunda. Valladolid, España.

Dizon, Eusebio et al. (5 October 1999). Southeast Asian Protohistoric Archaeology at Porac, Pampanga, Central Luzon, Philippines. Mid-Year Progress Report. Archaeological Studies Program. University of the Philippines at Diliman, Quezon City, Philippines.

Esguerra, Domingo. (1663). Arte de la lengua bisaya de la Provincia de Leyte. . . . Tiene enxeridas algvnas advertencias de la lengua de Zebú, y Bool: las de Zebú señaladas con la letra Z, y las de Bool con la letra B, y juntamente algunos adverbios con su vso para hablar con elegancia. Manila: Compañia de Jesus.

Fansler, Dean S. (1921). Filipino Popular Tales. Lancaster, Pennsylvania: American Folklore Society.

Francisco, Juan R. (1971). The Philippines and India: Essays in Ancient Cultural Relations. Mandaluyong, Rizal, Philippines: Premium Printing Press, Inc.

Francisco, Juan R. (1973). Philippine Paleography. Quezon City, Philippines: Linguistic Society of the Philippines.

Francisco, Juan R. and Han, Benjamin A. (1981). SEAMEO Project in Archeology and Fine Arts: Country report of the Philippines. In Studies on Srivijaya. Jakarta, Indonesia: Pusat Penelitan Arkeologi Nasional.

Gardner, Fletcher. (1869). Philippine Indic Studies: Fletcher Gardner. (2005 online ed.) Ann Arbor, Michigan: University of Michigan Library. Retrieved March 28, 2012 from http://quod.lib.umich.edu/p/phil-amer/AQQ3480.0001.001?view=toc.

Gerona, Lino. (2011 November 15). Conversations of Kapampangan Kulitan Pre-Hispanic Script. In DILA: United non-Tagalogs. Retrieved March 23, 2012 from http://groups.yahoo.com/group/DILA/message/24320.

Gueraiche, William. (2004). Quezon, an opportunistic nationalist? In Pilipinas, No. 42. Retrieved June 6, 2009 from http://www.scribd.com/doc/5999916/Quezon-An-Opportunistic-Nationalist-By-William-Gueraiche.

Henson, Mariano A. (1965). The Province of Pampanga and Its Towns: A.D. 1300-1965. 4th ed. revised. Angeles City: Mariano A. Henson.

Hikone Castle Museum (彦根城博物館). (1991 May 13). Daimyō no kakushiki o shimesu hittō dōgu ~ Ruson tsubo katsuyū yonmimi tsubo (大名の格式を示す筆頭道具　〜呂宋壷　[褐釉四耳壷]）[Japanese language only]. In Hikone Castle Museum News 13. Retrieved March 23, 2012 from http://longlife.city.hikone.shiga.jp/museum/letter/1301.html.

Hilario, Zoilo. (1962) Báyung Súnis. [Typescript].

Joosten, Leo. (2001). Kamus Batak Toba-Indonesia. Medan: Penerbit Bina Media.

Lacson, Evangelina Hilario. (1984). Kapampangan Writing: A Selected Compendium and Critique. Manila: National Historical Institute.

Lacson, Ariel. (1993 July 7). Kapampangan still alive and kicking. In Manila Bulletin.

Larkin, John A. (1972). The Pampangans: Colonial Society in a Philippine Province. 1993 Philippine Edition. Quezon City: New Day Publishers.

Ledyard, Gari K. (1998). The Korean Language Reform of 1446. Seoul: Shingu munhwasa.

Loarca, Miguel de. (1583) Relacion de las Yslas Filipinas. In E. Blair and J. Robertson, eds. and trans. The Philippine Islands, 1493-1898, volume 5, page 34 – 187.

Loeb, Edwin M. (1935). Sumatra: Its History and People. Wien: Verlag der Institut für Volkerkunde der Universitat Wien. [1989 ed.] Singapore: Oxford University Press.

Kitano, Hiroaki. (1997). Kapampangan. In Gary, Jane and Carl Rubino (eds.). Facts About the World's Languages: An Encyclopedia of the World's Major Languages: Past and Present. New York: H.W. Wilson

Malaiya, Yashwant (1997a). Evolution of Indian Scripts. In Languages and Scripts of India. Retrieved August 24, 1997 from http://www.cs.colostate.edu/~malaiya/images/brah11.gif.

Malaiya, Yashwant (1997b). Evolution of Southeast Asian Scripts. In Languages and Scripts of India. Retrieved August 24, 1997 from http://www.cs.colostate.edu/~malaiya/scripts.html.

Malaiya, Yashwant (1997c). Korean Script: Controversy about invention. In Languages and Scripts of India. Retrieved August 24, 1997 from http://www.cs.colostate.edu/~malaiya/korean.txt.

Mallat, Jean. (1846). Les Philippines: histoire, geographie, mœurs, agriculture, industrie, commerce des colonies Espagnoles dans l'Oceanie. Paris: Arthus Bertrand. [English ed. 1998] Santillan, P. and Castrence, L. (Transl.), Manila: National Historical Institute.

Manlapaz, Edna Zapanta. (1981). Kapampangan Literature: A Historical Survey and Anthology. Quezon City: Ateneo de Manila University Press.

Mantawe, Herb. (1998). Ethnic Cleansing in the Philippines. [2012 March 11 ed.]. Retrieved March 23, 2012 from http://dila.ph/ethnic.pdf.

Marcilla, Cipriano M. (1895). Estudio de los Antiguos Alfabetos Filipinos. Malabon: Tipo-Litografia del Asilo de Huérfanos.

Marche, Alfred. (1887). Luçon et Palaouan: Six Années de Voyages aux Philippines. Paris: Hachette.

Marsden, William. (1810). The History of Sumatra, containing an account of the government, laws, customs, and manners of the native inhabitants, with a description of the natural productions, and a relation of the ancient political state of that island. London: William Marsden.

Martinez, David C. (2004). A Country of Our Own: Partitioning the Philippines. Los Angeles, California, USA: Bisaya Books.

Mas, Sinibaldo de (1843). Informe sobre el estado de las Islas Filipinas en 1842. Madrid. Vol 1 retrieved March 26, 2012 from http://books.google.com.ph/books?id=rbM9AAAAIAAJ&printsec=frontcover&source=gbs_ge_summary_r&cad=0#v=onepage&q&f=false and Vol. 2 from http://books.google.com.ph/books/reader?id=RLM9AAAAIAA-J&printsec=frontcover&output=reader&pg=GBS.PP7.

Mi Guangjiang, Hajji Noor Deen. (2007). Official Website of Hajji Noor Deen. Retrieved 2012 March 16 from http://www.hajinoordeen.com/about.html.

Mi Guangjiang, Hajji Noor Deen. (2010). Arabic Calligraphy in the Chinese Tradition: The Art of Hajji Noor Deen Mi Guangjiang. Gansu, China: Gansu People's Press.

Miller, Christopher Ray. (2010 July 22). Transcription of Kapampangan Baybayin signatures appearing in two 1615 contracts tagged "Martinez de Rojo 1615", originally given to Jean-Paul Potet by Antoon Postma. [PDF document] retrieved through personal communication, July 10, 2011.

Miller, Christopher Ray. (2011 March 11). Indonesian and Philippine Scripts and extensions not yet encoded or proposed for encoding in Unicode as of version 6.0: A report for the Berkley Script Encoding Initiative. Retrieved March 23, 2012 from http://www.unicode.org/notes/tn35/indonesian-philippine.pdf.

Miller, Christopher Ray. (2011 December 2). Filipino Cultural Heritage in the UST Archives: Baybayin scripts in 17th century land deeds. A slide presentation at the University of Santo Tomas. [PDF document] retrieved March 12, 2012 from http://dl.dropbox.com/u/46259272/Chris%20Miller%20UST%20presentation%2020111202.pdf.

Miller, Christopher Ray. (2011 December 8). Linguistic insight into the history of Philippine script: graphonomic structure - sociolinguistic variation - contact phenomena. A paper presented at the 11th Philippine Linguistic Congress, UP Diliman, Quezon City, Philippines. [PDF document] retrieved March 13, 2012 from http://dl.dropbox.com/u/46259272/Miller%20PLC%20Baybayin%202011-12-08.pdf.

Miller, Christopher Ray. (2011 December 14). Redrawings of three 17th century Kapampangan signatures from the Manila Archdiocesan Archives. In Facebook [KULITAN (Indigenous Kapampangan Script)]. Retrieved December 16, 2011 from https://www.facebook.com/photo.php?fbid=10150439537433196&set=o.267202316630290&type=1&ref=nf.

Miller, Christopher Ray. (2012 February 18). The Nāgāri origin of the Sumatran and Sulawesi script: The Philippine connection. A paper presented at the Yale Indonesian Forum. [PDF document] retrieved March 15, 2012 from http://dl.dropbox.com/u/46259272/Yale%20Indonesian%20Forum%20presentation%202012-02-18.pdf.

Miller, Christopher Ray. (2012 April 8). On the difference between Kulitan and Baybayin. In Facebook [KULITAN (Indigenous Kapampangan Script)]. Retrieved 2012 April 8 from https://www.facebook.com/photo.php?fbid=3570214855545&set=o.267202316630290&type=1&theater.

Morga, Antonio de. (1609) Sucesos de las Islas Filipinas. Obra publicada en Mejico el año de 1609 nuevamente sacada a luz y anotada por Jose Rizal y precedida de un prologo del Prof. Fernando Blumentritt, Impresion al offset de la Edicion Anotada por Rizal, Paris 1890. [Reprinted 1991] Manila, Philippines: National Historical Institute.

Morrow, Paul. (2002). Baybayin ~ The Ancient Script of the Philippines. Retrieved November 25, 2008 from http://www.mts.net/~pmorrow/bayeng1.htm.

Morrow, Paul. (2005). Palaeographic Chart of the Philippine Islands. In Baybayin ~ The Ancient Script of the Philippines. Retrieved March 26, 2012 from http://www.mts.net/~pmorrow/paterno.htm.

Morrow, Paul. (2009 June 16 - 30). Da Bathala Code. In The Pilipino Express, Vol. 5, No.12. PDF format retrieved March 28, 2012 from http://www.pilipino-express.com/pdfs/inotherwords/Da%20Bathala%20Code.pdf

Morrow, Paul. (2010 June 1). Jose Rizal and the Filipino Language. In The Pilipino Express, Vol. 5, No.12. PDF format retrieved March 28, 2012 from http://www.pilipino-express.com/history-a-culture/in-otherwords/852-rizal-and-the-filipino-language.html.

Murillo Velarde, Pedro. (1744). Mapa de las islas Filipinas. In The Norman B. Leventhal Map Center at the Boston Public Library. Retrieved March 8, 2012 from http://www.leventhalmapcenter.org/id/11077.

Nakano, Satoshi. (1999). Appeasement and Coercion. In Ikehata, Setsuho and Jose, Rico Trota (eds). The Philippines Under Japan: Occupation Policy and Reaction. Quezon City: Ateneo de Manila University Press.

National Historical Institute (NHI). (1990). Filipinos in History. 2 vols. Manila: National Historical Institute.

National Script Act, House Bill No. 4395, 15th Congress, 1st Regular Session. (2011 March 16).

Nupsa, Yavre Canda. (2011 September 21). Understanding the Basics of Kulitan (The Kapampangan Writing System) [Video file]. Retrieved March 31, 2012 from http://www.youtube.com/watch?v=3sOoQZZd-3pg.

Pandey, Anshuman. (2012 February 8). Preliminary Proposal to Encode Siddham in ISO/IEC 10646. PDF Document retrieved March 16, 2012 from http://std.dkuug.dk/JTC1/SC2/WG2/docs/n4185.pdf.

Panganiban, Jose Villa. (1972). Diksyunaryo-Tesauro Pilipino-Ingles. Quezon City: Manlapaz Publishing Co.

Pangilinan, Michael R. M. [as Siuálâ ding Meángûbié]. (1995). Pamagkulit King Kekatamung Matuang Kasulatan. In Ing Susi, 6:1:24-25.

Pangilinan, Michael R.M. (2000). Dalit nang Ápûng Sínukûan. Kulitan verse [Manuscript]. Verse in Latin script [Typescript].

Pangilinan, Michael R. M. (2002). Matuâng Súlat Kapampángan. [PowerPoint slides]. A lecture presented to the students and teachers of Kapampangan Culture (YKAMP) at the end of every semester from the years 2002-2004, Holy Angel University, Angeles City.

Pangilinan, Michael R.M. (2006a) Kapampángan or Capampáñgan: Settling the Dispute on the Kapampángan Romanized Orthography. A paper presented at the 10th International Conference on Austronesian Linguistiics, Puerto Princesa, Palawan, Philippines. January 2006.

Pangilinan, Michael R.M. (2006b). The Importance of Diacritical Marks in Romanized Kapampangan. A paper presented at the 10th International Conference on Austronesian Linguistiics, Puerto Princesa, Palawan, Philippines. January 2006.

Pangilinan, Michael R. M. (2008). Súlat Kapampángan. [PowerPoint slides]. A lecture presented to the Pampanga Arts Guild, the Pampanga Tattoo Community and the Maharlika Artists and Writers Federation, Aftershack Gallery, Balibago, Angeles City, September 10, 17 & 24, 2008. (2011) Revised edition presented to the CASEd Faculty at Holy Angel University, September 30, 2011.

Pangilinan, Michael R.M. (2009a). Assessing the current status of the Kapampangan "pre-Hispanic" script. A paper presented at the 11th International Conference on Austronesian Linguistics, June 21 - 25, 2009, Aussois, France.

Pangilinan, Michael R.M. (2009b). Kapampangan lexical borrowing from Tagalog: endangerment rather than enrichment. A paper presented at the 11th International Conference on Austronesian Linguistics, June 21 - 25, 2009, Aussois, France.

Postma, Antoon. (1991). The Laguna Copper-Plate Inscription (LCI): A Valuable Philippine Document. In National Museum Papers, Vol. 2, No. 1, 1-25.

Potet, Jean-Paul. (2012 April 8). Comment on the image for the brush work of the word 'ualu'. In Facebook [KULITAN (Indigenous Kapampangan Script)]. Retrieved 2012 April 8 from https://www.facebook.com/photo.php?fbid=3570214855545&set=o.267202316630290&type=1&theater.

San Agustin, Gaspar de. (1699). Conquistas de las Islas Philipinas 1565-1615. [1998 Bilingual Ed.: Spanish & English] Translated by Luis Antonio Mañeru. Published by Pedro Galende, OSA: Intramuros, Manila.

San Antonio, Juan Francisco de. (1738-1744). Cronicas de la apostolic provincial de S. Gregorio de religiosos de n.s.p. San Francisco en las islas Philipinas, China, Japon. Sampaloc: Juan del Sotillo.

Santiago, Luciano P.R. (1990a) The Houses of Lakandula, Matanda, and Soliman [1571-1898]: Genealogy and Group Identity. In Philippine Quarterly of Culture and Society, Vol. 18, No. 1.

Santiago, Luciano P.R. (1990b). The Filipinos Indios Encomenderos [ca. 1620-1711]: Genealogy and Group Identity. In Philippine Quarterly of Culture and Society, Vol. 18, No. 3.

Santiago, Luciano. (2002). Laying the Foundations: Kapampangan Pioneers in the Philippine Church 1592-2001. Angeles City, Philippines: Juan D. Nepomuceno Center for Kapampangan Studies, Holy Angel University.

Santos, Norman de los. (2010 January 12). Galit sa Kulit. In Baybayin Modern Fonts (Anak Bathala Project). Retrieved March 23, 2012 from http://nordenx.blogspot.com/2010/01/galit-sa-kulit.html.

Santos, Norman de los. (2011 August 2). Baybayin Kapampangan. In Baybayin Modern Fonts (Anak Bathala Project). Retrieved March 23, 2012 from http://nordenx.blogspot.com/2011/08/baybayin-kapampangan.html.

Santos, Norman de los. (2011 August 28). Kulitan Angulo Typepad. In Baybayin Modern Fonts (Anak Bathala Project). Retrieved March 23, 2012 from http://nordenx.blogspot.com/2011/08/kulitan-angulo-typepad.html.

Satyawati, Sulaiman. (1980). The History and Art of Srivijaya. In The Art of Srivijaya [Subhadradis Diskul ed.]. Paris: UNESCO.

Satyawati, Sulaiman. (1981). Research on Srivijaya History and Art History. In Studies on Srivijaya. Jakarta, Indonesia: Pusat Penelitan Arkeologi Nasional.

Scott, William Henry. (1984). Prehispanic Source Materials for the Study of Philippine History. Quezon City: New Day Publishers.

Scott, William Henry. (1994). Barangay: Sixteenth-Century Philippine

Culture and Society, Quezon City: Ateneo de Manila University Press.

Tauchi Yonesaburo (田内米三郎). (1853). Toukikou (陶器考: Investigations of Pottery). English Translation in Cole, Fay-Cooper. (1912) Chinese Pottery in the Philippines. Field Museum of Natural History Anthropological Series, Vol. 12 (1), Chicago.

Tayag, Katoks (Renato). (1985). The Vanishing Pampango Nation. Recollections & Digressions. Escolta, Manila: Philnabank Club c/o Philippine National Bank.

Terami-Wada, Motoe. (1999). The Filipino Volunteer Armies. In Ikehata, Setsuho and Jose, Rico Trota (eds). The Philippines Under Japan: Occupation Policy and Reaction. Quezon City: Ateneo de Manila University Press.

Tolentino, Guillermo E. (1937). Ağ Wika at Baybayiğ Tagalog. Maynila: Guillermo E. Tolentino.

Verzosa, Paul Rodriguez (1939). Pangbansang Titik nang Pilipinas (Philippine National Writing). Manila (no publisher).

Wade, Geoff. (1993). On the Possible Cham Origin of the Philippine Scripts. In Journal of Southeast Asian Studies 24, 1 (March 1993): 44-87.

Wade, Geoff. [tr.] (2005) Southeast Asia in the Ming Shi-lu: an open access resource. Singapore: Asia Research Institute and the Singapore E-Press, National University of Singapore. http://epress.nus.edu.sg/msl/place/1062

Wang, Teh-Ming (王德明). (1989). Sino Suluan Historical Relations in Ancient Texts. (Doctoral dissertation, University of the Philippines, Diliman, Quezon City, 2001). Unpublished typescript.

Wang, Zhenping. (2008). Reading Song-Ming Records on the Pre-colonial History of the Philippines. 東アジア文化交渉研究 創刊号. [Higashi Ajia bunka kōshō kenkyū, No.1] (2008): 249-260.

West, Andrew. (2006 November 25). Christian Tombstones of Zayton. In BabelStone. Retireved March 28, 2012 from http://babelstone.blogspot.com/2006/11/christian-tombstones-of-zayton.html.

West, Andrew. (2006 December 21). Měnggǔ Zìyùn (蒙古字韻) "Mongolian Letters Arranged by Rhyme". In Phags-pa Script: Menggu Ziyun. Retrieved March 28, 2012 from http://www.babelstone.co.uk/Phags-pa/MengguZiyun.html.

Yijing (義淨). (695). 南海寄歸內法傳 (An Account of Buddhism as Practiced in the South Seas, 671-695 C.E.). Partial translation courtesy of Angus Ling, September 12, 2003.

Zhang Xie (張燮). (1617). Dong Xi Yang Gao [東西洋考] (A study of the Eastern and Western Oceans). http://www.lib.kobe-u.ac.jp/directory/sumita/5A-161/index.html, Volume (分冊) 3:9.

zhaijia1987 (2010 November 11). Cóng dà míngkūn yú wànguó tú kàn lìshǐ (從大明坤輿萬國圖看歷史) "A look at history based on the map of the Great Ming Empire". In Baidu Tieba (百度貼吧). Retrieved April 4, 2012 from http://tieba.baidu.com/f?kz=932527323.

PITALUKÎAN
Index

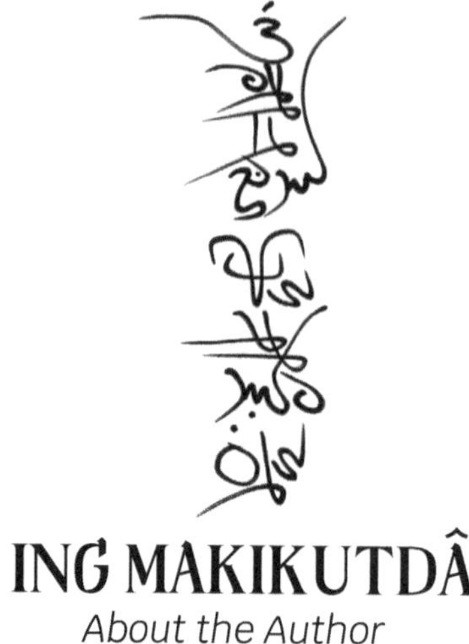

ING MAKIKUTDÂ
About the Author

SIUÁLÂ DING MEÁNGÛBIÉ, from the Kapampángan words *siuálâ*, which means "voice", and *meángúbié*, a polite reference to the dead, was born in Angeles City as Michael Raymon Tayag-Manaloto Pangilinan, but grew up in his mother's hometown of Magalang at the foot of the mystical Bunduk Aláya, home of the Kapampángan sun god, Ápung Sínukuan.

Mike Pangilinan, as he is now popularly known, is an internationally recognized expert on Kapampangan Philosophy, History, Language and Culture whose works have been published and broadcasted in international journals and conferences. His ideas and activities which began in the late 1980s paved the way for the Kapampangan cultural boom of the 2000s and served as the conceptual basis for the creation of the Center for Kapampangan Studies, the First International Conference on Kapampangan Studies, the first academic course on Kapampangan Studies and numerous Kapampangan cultural organizations which eventually mushroomed all over the province and the internet.

Acknowledged as a "living Kapampangan culture resource center" by his peers, Mike Pangilinan became a recipient of the prestigious Most Outstanding Kapampangan Award (MOKA) in the field of Culture in 2010. In 2011, he was recognized as the "Father of Filipino Calligraphy" by none other than the "Father of New Philippine Historiography," Zeus Salazar. Pangilinan is one of the few Kapampángan culture-bearers who can still read and write in the indigenous Kapampángan script, *Kulitan*. In 2013, Mike Pangilinan became a visiting professor at the Tokyo University of Foreign Studies (TUFS) in Tokyo, Japan. He later took up a number of post graduate units in Linguistics at the Heinrich Heine Universität Düsseldorf (HHU) in Germany. Upon returning to Ángeles City, Mike Pangilinan received the lifetime achievement award, *Talasínup king Singsing*, from the government and people of Angeles City in 2016 for his lifelong contribution to Kapampángan research. He also became head of the Ágúman Sínúpan Singsing, Inc., an NGO dedicated to the research, documentation, protection and promotion of Kapampángan cultural heritage. In 2019, he received the PAMANA (*Págmaragul at Maténákang Ának ning Ángeles*) Award which honors the outstanding sons and daughters of Angeles City. Mike Pangilinan has recently stepped down as Program Director of the Ágúman Sínúpan Singsing, Inc. in June 2023 and now currently serves it as one of its senior advisers.